FROM
THE PLOW
TO THE
PULPIT

A Spiritual Autobiography by

TOMMIE F. HARPER

Edited by

Elizabeth Harper Neeld

CENTERPOINT PRESS

1986

Text/Cover Design by Luis Gonzalez

Cover: Quilt by Willie Harper   Quilt Pattern: Rocky Road

Library of Congress Cataloging-in-Publication Data

Harper, Tommie F., 1908–
  From the plow to the pulpit.
  1. Harper, Tommie F., 1908–   2. Church of
God (Cleveland, Tenn.)—Clergy—Biography.   3. Church
of God—United States—Clergy—Biography.   I. Neeld,
Elizabeth Cowan, 1940–   II. Title.
BX7034.Z8H37   1986   289.9 [B]   86-9656
ISBN 0-937897-77-9 (Softcover)

for Rachel

THE GREAT INVOCATION

From the point of Light
    within the Mind of God
Let light stream forth into
    the minds of men.
Let Light descend on Earth.

From the point of Love
    within the Heart of God
Let love stream forth into
    the hearts of men.
May Christ return to Earth.

From the centre where the
    Will of God is known
Let purpose guide the little
    wills of men—
The purpose which the Masters know and serve.

From the centre which we call
    the race of men
Let the Plan of Love and Light
    work out.
And may it seal the door where evil dwells.

Let Light and Love and Power restore the Plan on Earth.

Anonymous

TABLE OF CONTENTS

INTRODUCTION   Reverend Ray H. Hughes

PREFACE   Elizabeth Harper Neeld

PART I: PREPARATION

PART II: TRAINING

PART III: SERVICE

PART IV: THE HARVEST

EPILOGUE

INTRODUCTION TO THE
CENTENNIAL EDITION

Over the past 100 years the Church has produced some powerful preachers, preachers who have delivered their souls without fear or favor. These preachers have changed the world and established a Church which now has a ministry world-wide. One such man among the thousands is Tommie Harper. For forty-eight of the 100 years of the existence of the Church of God, he has ministered faithfully as a pastor, evangelist, and administrator.

Having known him personally, I have observed the hand of God upon his ministry in a very definite way. It has been evident to all of those who have come under the influence of his ministry that God gave him special ministerial gifts and made him a vessel unto honor prepared for His work.

Possibly this man could best be introduced in Biblical terms:

> Tommie Harper: a man full of the Holy Ghost and power, separated by the Spirit, and anointed of God for the work whereunto he was called; a minister of the full gospel who fed the flock of God over which the Holy Ghost made him overseer, whose speech and whose preaching was not with enticing words of man's wisdom, but in demonstration of the Spirit; and who has the testimony among his peers that he pleased God.

This book is the life story of such a man. In reading the life story of Tommie Harper, one sees what God can do with a man who is wholly and unreservedly dedicated to Him. While the book is about an individual, it honors God and shows forth the depth of riches of divine grace.

Reverend Ray H. Hughes, President
The Church of God School of Theology

PREFACE

I t was a strange assignment.

A hundred and fifty of us—writers, editors, newspaper and magazine executives—from many parts of the world had gathered in a beautiful university conference center to spend twelve days looking at the current state of affairs in the field of publishing.

One afternoon, late in the course, the seminar director said:

"Tonight when you go to your rooms, please set aside a few minutes to do this assignment:

Ask yourself, 'What do I want to have accomplished before I die?'

After you have thought about this question, please write your own obituary."

The seminar director's purpose, I suppose, was to have us think about those books we had not yet written, those projects we had put aside, those dreams we had not yet achieved. Perhaps if we remembered all these things, we would leave the publishing conference with a renewed commitment to reach new pinnacles in our work.

But the assignment had a far different effect on me.

Sitting in my room that night, I pondered the answers to questions like these: What do I want to have done before I die? Of the things I have already done, what matters? What is the point to how I spend the hours of my days?

As I considered these questions, I knew that a review of any honors and recognition I might have earned would be hollow after I was dead. I knew those things that keep me busy everyday—the hustle and bustle of daily affairs— certainly would not be what I wanted to be remembered for. I knew that a list of the books I had written would be unimportant unless those books had made a contribution to people's lives.

In being asked to write my own obituary, I had to take stock of what really mattered. This inquiry allowed me to reaffirm the values I would like to be known for after I was dead. And these values, I realized, were simple values. They were ancient values. And they were values I had learned from my father.

That evening I could almost hear his voice reading the Bible from the pulpit:

Thou shalt love the Lord thy God with all thy heart, and with all thy soul, and with all thy mind.
Thou shalt love thy neighbour as thyself.

I knew then that in my obituary it would be enough if someone wrote: *She served God . . . she contributed to others . . . she was her father's daughter.* What had been just a daily assignment in a publishing course had returned me home.

*   *   *

Now, there was not much evidence when Tommie Harper was growing up in the red-clay hills of middle Georgia that he would even live to be a grown man, much less live to become a man of God who would have a major impact on his children and on thousands of others to whom he ministered along the way.

Tommie's idol was his father. His father was honest, but he was rough. Tommie wanted to grow up to be just like him.

The Harper family during Tommie's childhood was not what you would call religiously inclined. If his parents went to church at all, it was to the yearly protracted meeting. Tommie did not attend. By the time he was a teen-ager, Tommie's path was set. He wanted no part of God.

Yet, even as the Harper family worked in the sandy soil, took the cotton to the gin, cut wood and hauled it into town, God's spirit was hovering over them. The unfathomable purpose of God's Plan was at work. Tommie was being prepared to do God's work.

Who would have thought on that July night in 1938 when he headed over to the pasture where the visiting evangelist was preaching a revival that, instead of cutting the ropes on the tent as he had planned to do, Tommie Harper would find himself in the mourner's bench?

But that is getting ahead of the story. . . .

Elizabeth Harper Neeld

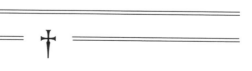

PART
I

PREPARATION
1908–1932

*But ask now the beasts, and they shall teach thee;
and the fowls of the air, and they shall tell thee: Or speak
to the earth, and it shall teach thee: and the fishes of the
sea shall declare unto thee. Who knoweth not in all these
that the hand of the Lord hath wrought this? In whose
hand is the soul of every living thing, and the breath of
all mankind.*

Job 12: 7–10

Tommie Frank Harper was born on
April 30, 1908, in the rural community of Brooks, Georgia, population 210.

The first decade of the 20th century was momentous. Admiral Peary, on his sixth attempt, finally reached the North Pole. Oklahoma was admitted to the Union as the forty-sixth state, and Oliver Wendell Holmes was appointed to the United States Supreme Court. McKinley had been re-elected President, assassinated, and replaced by Theodore Roosevelt. Now, in 1908, William Taft had just been elected President of the United States.

In San Francisco, the great earthquake had caused major damage, starting fires which raged for three days. A yellow fever epidemic had killed 400 people in New Orleans. The first baseball World Series had been played. The first movie attempting to tell a story had been seen on the silver screen. The Model T had gone into mass production; and the first automobile trip from coast to coast had been completed, taking two months and nine days to travel the distance from San Francisco to New York. Orville Wright had made the first flight in a powered, heavier-than-air machine, a plane designed with his brother Wilbur.

All this, and the century was just beginning!

Closer to home, forty miles away, in Atlanta. The first horseless carriage had appeared on the city's streets, and the first accident had already occurred. The auto ran into the rear wheel of a surrey; the driver of the horseless carriage and the two occupants of the horse-drawn carriage were thrown to the ground. (By the year following Tommie Harper's birth, 150,000 people would be attending the Automobile Show of 1909, hosted by Asa Chandler, who was making good with the little soft drink concern he had recently purchased, the Coca-Cola Company.)

*The Atlanta race riot of 1906 had raged for three
days, with seven dead and over seventy injured. The
Georgia legislature had abolished the convict labor leas-
ing system, known for its harsh conditions and extreme
brutality, and had adopted a literacy test and property
ownership as qualifications for voting. The state had
also adopted a prohibition law. Alcohol could not be le-
gally consumed anywhere in Georgia. "Next Wednesday
[January 1, 1908], there will be closed in Atlanta under
the state prohibition law eighty-six whiskey saloons,
twenty-three beer saloons, twenty-one wholesale liquor
houses and two wholesale beer houses."*

All this was happening in the outside world; but it
might as well have been in another galaxy as far as the
Harper family living in Brooks, Fayette County, Georgia,
were concerned. Even though they lived only forty miles
below Atlanta, they were not part of this bustling, improving, advancing, turbulent, vigorous outside world.

What mattered to the Harpers was what happened on their farm. Not because they deliberately isolated themselves, but because they had to survive. Their
eyes were on the next row of cotton and the next stalk of
corn. They were attached to the land.

There might be some trickling in of outside news
from people who went up to Atlanta or from the tri-
weekly newspaper that arrived at the Harper farm. But
inventions and advancements did not reach the red-clay
hills of middle Georgia until long after they had appeared in Atlanta; and, when they did arrive, they came
as the result of a combination of hard work and good
luck. Music, for instance, became a part of the Harper
household when the four children—Nonie, Tommie,
Blanche, and Nannie—sold flower seeds around the
countryside to earn a big gray Gramophone. As a result
of the prosperous cotton-growing years from 1916 to
1918, Frank Harper was able to buy the family's first car,
a Whippet Overland Touring Car.

What got the Harpers' attention and absorbed all their energies were matters of daily existence: The boll weevil destroying the cotton crop, ice storms freezing the animals caught out in the brush, Granddad John Harper stumbling in a daze in the field and never being able to farm again. Their concerns were for repairing the wagon wheels and plows in their blacksmith shop, for resoling the old work boots and repairing the mule harnesses around the fireplace at night, for welcoming the peddler Rosenblum to the table when he came through in his gypsy wagon, bringing the desperately needed pails and buckets, needles and thread.

What made the Harper men happy were the peaches fermenting to make brandy, corn mash to make pure corn whiskey, tobacco to twist into chewing plugs, apples to dry for the winter, hogs to kill for fresh meat, squirrels to hunt which would be served with hot dumplings. What gave joy to Willie Harper and the girls in the family were new gingham for dresses and denim for overalls, a new Sunday hat, visits with the neighbors, and cotton bringing a high enough price so they could finally buy a fancy White treadle sewing machine.

Life at Harper Mountain revolved around the 260 acres they farmed with six mules and whatever collection of men and boys they could round up to do the work. During planting, chopping, and harvesting times, the women, too, helped in the fields and then went home to put dinner or supper on the table.

The day Tommie Harper was born, April 30, 1908, in the log house built up high on big pillars of rocks brought up from Flint River, the family's most pressing concern was an act of nature. Five days before, a tornado had swept through, barely missing the Harper homeplace. The storm, which touched down in the town of Griffin, fifteen miles away, killed more than 200 people before losing its force. The tornado had done extensive damage to the Harper's crops, but Frank and Willie had *already collected what they would use to pay old Dr. Noah Gable for delivering their new baby, things provided by the farm: canned vegetables, cured meat, chickens, and some dried beef.*

It was in this austere, demanding, unrelenting environment that Tommie Harper grew up; and he grew up a match to that environment. But let's hear him tell the story.

THE DAY I GOT MY MULE

4:00 AM. Still dark outside.

Nonie and I slept in the room that had been built out on the front porch. We heard Papa outside our door.

"Ok, boys, no time to stay in bed. There's a crop to plant and a crop to harvest and no one to do the work but you. So, let us go and get the job done."

We were running a six-horse farm. This

means that there were six mules working in the fields every day. Papa's farm was 160 acres and Granddad's was a hundred. We were farming all of it—Papa, Granddad, Nonie, Dave (our cousin that Mama and Papa had taken in), and me. With Sweet Charity and her six children, who were sharecroppers on the place.

My Granddad was still a regular plowhand, so he was out with us in the field. We were plowing young cotton. Suddenly, Granddad had an attack. He was unable to walk without a stagger, and sometimes he would fall. This left us one mule short.

After we got Granddad back to the house and returned to the field, I picked up my hoe and started back chopping cotton.

But Papa said, "Tom, can you handle old Ada and a plow stock?" (Ada was a big, one-eyed, broken-down mule that weighed over 1200 pounds.)

I answered quickly. "Yes, Sir!"

Papa fixed the plow handles to fit a little boy (I was a runt until I was way up in my teens) and, with that 1200-pound mule in front of me, in my mind I became a man!

I was put bustin' middles in front of five plows. The ground was hard, and it was difficult to get enough dirt up around the shoots of young cotton and corn. Someone needed to run a small scrape through the middles to loosen up the soil before the plows came along to make the furrows. To have a plow scrape go ahead bustin' the middles was a job that had to be done, and to have that scrape stay ahead of five plows meant that somebody had to stay on his toes.

Old Ada was a slow plow mule, and I was new at the job. The other plows caught up with me all day long the first day. Papa would help me get ahead, and then I'd go for it on my own again. But the plows would still catch up. That continued on the second day. And then the third. Finally, Papa asked me again, "Tom, you sure you can or want to take Granddad's place in the field?"

"If you will give me the mule that Granddad plowed, I can stay ahead of the others," was my reply.

Papa thought about this for a little while and then called to Dave who was plowing the mule I wanted, a young six-year-old mule that was what was called a fast-stepper. "Dave, give that mule to Tom. You take Ada." My new mule was easy to handle, and all you had to do was just touch her with the line to get more out of her. From that day on, the other five plows could never catch up with me.

Now that I had my own mule and was a full-time plowhand, I wanted to do everything the way Papa and the other men did.

Something I could not understand was why the other fellows plowing in the same field that I was in would get wet with sweat and I wouldn't. It embarrassed me always to have a dry shirt! Maybe they would think I wasn't working as hard as they were.

Finally, I hit on a way to get my shirt wet. While no one was around, I would take the water jug and pour water on my head and let it run down on my shirt. Then I'd look like all the rest. But this would not last long. The hot sun would dry out my shirt, and I would have to pour on more water. I found out later that spring, when we were plowing corn and it got waist- to head-high, that I did not have to pour water on myself to get wet. Then the work was so hard that I had to pour water in while the sweat poured out!

When some farmer would drive by and ask Papa if he had hired a man to take Grand-dad's place in the field, I'd hear him say, "No, Tom has taken his place." The farmer would say, "But he is too small to do much." Papa would answer, "Tom's a good worker, and I can count on him."

That did make an eight-year-old feel like a man.

The Harpers began picking cotton in
September or October and hoped to get done by Christ-
mas. They tried to make thirty to thirty-five bales, and
this required picking as much as 52,500 pounds of cot-
ton. (Fifteen hundred pounds were required to make one
500-pound bale of ginned cotton.) An adult who was a
good cotton picker could pick 700 to 750 pounds in a
day. Children, of course, picked less. Everybody was put
in the field because the cotton needed to be picked before
winter rains and cold set in. The weather was a serious
consideration.

Cottonpicking stopped, however, the afternoon
the scales in the field showed that the first 1500 pounds
had been picked. That load would go to the gin tomorrow
to be sold for seed; the family would have some cash for
the first time in many months.

PAPA AND I GO TO THE GIN

E very year, when October came, we
would pick our first load of cotton. It was a time
of celebration! Everybody would get out in the
field to pick because it took 1500 pounds of cotton
to fill the wagon.

This first load of cotton always went to the
gin immediately to be sold for seed. (Cotton seeds

were used to make yellow cotton-seed meal for cows, fertilizer, and cotton-seed oil that we'd use on our harnesses and that was put in paint. The man at the gin would sell the seeds to a big company up in Atlanta.) We'd get maybe $10 or $15 for the seed in this first load of cotton. This cash was the first money we'd have gotten for months and months; it helped us get by until all the cotton was ginned and sold later on.

I always got to go with Papa to take the first cotton load to the gin at Senoia. Everybody would help load the wagon in the afternoon or at night, depending on when we finished picking the first 1500 pounds, and Papa and I would leave early the next morning. The whole family would come out and watch us leave. The field hands would be there, too. Everybody would be standing around the wagon in the yard. One kid would say, "Papa, bring me so and so," and another would say, "Papa, bring me so and so."

The 1500 pounds of cotton would be in the back of the wagon. Papa and I would be sitting tall on the seat. I loved that ride. I'd forget how much I hated to pick cotton. I'd forget all those mornings we had to start before daylight, before the sun came up over Harper Mountain. (You'd nearly freeze to death at the foot of that mountain.) I forgot everything except that Papa and I were taking the first load of cotton to the Senoia gin.

After Papa sold the cotton for seed and had money in his pocket, we'd go by Holberg's General Mercantile Store and Crooks Fish Market. We'd buy the same thing every year: a dime's worth of cheese and a nickel's worth of sweet crackers for our dinner and a mess of mullet fish, maybe six, seven, eight pounds, a stalk of bananas and a ring of cheese to take home. Everybody had a feast.

A WHIPPING THAT MAKES
ME WELL

That summer I got typhoid fever and was sick for several months. Dr. Noah Gable came to the house to take care of me. He gave Mama stern orders: "This boy is to eat nothing but milk, crackers, and apple butter."

Since Granddad was now too unsteady to go to the field, he was at the house every day.

Most of the time he sat out by the well making baskets for us to use when we picked cotton or corn. These were big baskets, over waist high, four feet across at the bottom, big enough to hold 200 to 250 pounds of cotton. He also made baskets that had handles on them; these would hold a half bushel to a bushel of corn. We used these when we fed the mules and the hogs.

Granddad made these baskets out of strips he cut out of white oak. He would rive the strips and trim them up real thin so he could handle them. He kept these strips soaking in a tub of water out by the well.

It was cottonpicking time, and everybody was needed out in the field, including Mama. So, every morning Mama would cook the family's dinner while she was cooking breakfast. Then she'd leave it on the stove when they went to the field.

Since I was sick, Mama left me with Granddad. I was supposed to stay in bed all day, eating my crackers and milk and apple butter. But as I got better, I'd slip through the kitchen (I'd be so hungry!), and I'd get a handful of beans out of the pot sitting on the stove.

Eating these beans would cause me to have a backset. The doctor would be called back out to the house. "It's something he's eating," the doctor would say. But nobody could figure out how that could be the case since all I was eating was milk, crackers, and apple butter.

While Granddad worked on his baskets, he was watching to see what it was that caused these backsets. One day he caught me eating the beans! I tried to run away, but he caught up with me at the well where he made those baskets. He first knocked me down and put his foot on the back of my neck. Then he took one of those white oak splits—and he didn't make a basket! He dusted the seat of my britches real good. From that time on I began to improve; and before winter was well on the way, I got well.

The white oak split did what the doctor couldn't do!

A COLD WINTER NIGHT

You never really rest on a farm. In good weather we were always out in the field. The work started in the fall when we turned under stubble. Then in the spring we started getting the land ready for planting.

We started planting such things as Irish potatoes the first dark night in February. Gardens were fixed and beans always planted on Good Friday. We planted some corn in March, then some in April. Our bottom land was never planted until the full moon in May.

We tried to get through picking cotton before Christmas, but if the weather was bad, we might not finish until March of the next year. We always got our corn in before Christmas. We would always have two cribs full, 300 or 400 bushels. When corngathering and cottonpicking were finished, woodcutting started. There were always 100 to 150 cords of wood to cut and stack.

We told time by the sun. When we wanted to know if it was time to go home for dinner, we'd take a step. If the toe of our shoe showed out from under the shadow of our wide-brimmed hat when we stepped, that meant it was 11:30 and time to go to the house to eat. At the end of the day, we just worked until there was no light to see by. Then we went in, threw the shucks or the feed to the stock, ate supper, sharpened hoes or fixed cotton sacks while the womenfolk cleaned up the kitchen and then everybody went straight to bed.

In bad weather we worked all the same. Nobody stopped when it rained or turned cold. We'd work in the blacksmith shop sharpening plows or repairing wagon wheels, in the barn mending harnesses, or in the corncrib shucking corn.

I started working in the blacksmith shop with Papa when I was about nine. Papa would show me how to fix a wagon wheel. It was time for me to learn to make and repair things around the farm.

"Break this wheel down, Tom. It's too loose to stay on the wagon anymore. Now, take the steel tire off it and work a piece of hickory wood around it. Tack it on there, and then heat that wagon steel rim and put it back on the wheel. You've got a new wheel out of it. Now all you have to do is make the spokes."

And we'd turn to shaving sticks to put new spokes in the wheel.

Papa always let us call it quits earlier in the day when it was cold and rainy. We headed to the house. I loved days like this because you could count on Mama to have a big plate of fried pies waiting when you got to the kitchen for supper. Mama would spend almost all day in the kitchen during bad weather, frying pies made out of the dried apples and peaches we stored out in the room on the porch. What a delicious smell on a rainy winter day!

When supper was over, the whole family went to sit in front of the fire in the big room where Granddad slept. Mama would sew patches on clothes or make new overalls and dresses by hand. Papa would put new half soles on our shoes or mend broken laces.

With the wind howling outside and everything about us cold except our front side facing the fire, we'd enjoy some baked sweet potatoes roasted in the fireplace and a big pan of peanuts which we had grown and which Mama had roasted that day. We would eat so many peanuts that the floor around us would be covered with hulls.

Granddad would cook johnnycakes before the fire. Johnnycakes were made with corn meal. A batter was made from the meal and put on a board that was made from white oak. One side would get brown in the fireplace, and then Granddad would turn the johnnycake over to brown the other side. We would then take the cake while it was hot and put butter on it with a little sugar or syrup. Then we'd put this in our mouths. That was eating!

Granddad would tell stories about his days in the Civil War. If we were lucky he'd bring out the gold-plated pistol he carried into battle at Franklin and Chickamauga and Missionary Ridge. Papa would tell hunting stories of running wildcats in the mountains, how an old bearcat could slip a whole pack of hounds. Everybody would reminisce about the time we had a big snow and went rabbit hunting with sticks and one single-shot 22 rifle.

I could never forget those cold winter nights, a big fire going, peanut hulls covering the floor, a pile of roasted sweet potatoes on the hearth waiting to be buttered. The johnnycakes will soon be ready. Don't call now. The family are busy with their most enjoyable time. The country boy is at home where he will tell you, "This is living."

GRANDDAD TELLS ABOUT THE CIVIL WAR

I loved to hear Granddad tell about the days when he fought in the Civil War. He joined the army in Franklin, Tennessee, and fought through Chattanooga, Missionary Ridge,

Chickamauga, and on to Atlanta, where he was wounded. He ended up in Jonesboro, a little piece out of Atlanta. From there he watched Sherman burn the city. By the time Granddad's wound healed, Sherman had marched to the sea in Savannah, and the war was over between the states.

"Tell me about Grandpa Martin," I'd beg Granddad. Asa Martin was Granddad's father-in-law. Father-in-law and son-in-law had fought in the Civil War.

"Well, Asa Martin and I came over from Ireland together," Granddad would say. "Settled in Virginia. The Martins bought a big plantation there. That's where I married your grandmother Susan, Asa's daughter. But Asa was more like my brother than my pa-in-law. We heard about a lot of land being available in Georgia, so four families who lived close together in Virginia moved down here: The Martins and Harpers, the Cobbs, and the Isons."

"You moved right here to Harper Mountain?" I'd ask?

"Yes, settled about two miles apart. And I picked out this spot right here. Settled among the Creek Indians. Bought this land you're sitting on right now from the Creeks. Used to trade with them when we first settled. Bought those clay dishes we eat on from the Indians. I remember when the tribe had a crossing down at Flint River."

"Where did Grandpa Martin fight in the war?" I'd ask.

And Granddad would answer, "He left for the war first, leaving me to oversee the crops and take care of the women here. We had lots more land then than we do today. Asa got captured and died in a Union prison in Rockford, Illinois. They said he died of typhoid fever, but we always thought he starved to death. Then when the troops got pinned down in Franklin, Tennessee . . . that's when I knew I had to join the war."

Then Granddad would start talking about the womenfolk of the family and what they did after he left to fight. I knew this story well, because we had been digging for Grandma's china and silver for years down in the little swamp-head behind the house where she remembered burying it. (As far as we know, nobody ever found it.)

"Your Grandma and her mother took the silver and china they prized so highly, and they buried it below the house before the Yankees came through. All the men were fighting in the army, and one old slave had stayed with the womenfolk. He cut the wood and brought in the water."

"During Sherman's march from Atlanta to Savannah, soldiers came through our section and stole all the horses that were left, leaving our womenfolk with one old broken-down, sway-backed mare. One day some stray soldiers came riding into the yard. They searched the whole place—the house and the barn. One of the soldiers came around the side of the house with six or eight chickens tied together in his hands. Then he went into the kitchen and cut down the only piece of meat the womenfolk had left, a cured ham. Then the soldier came on through the house to the front porch. Grandma Martin was standing out in the yard. The soldier came out with those chickens and that ham and said, 'Thank you, M'am. We'll just take these chickens and this ham.'"

"Grandma Martin said, 'That's the only piece of meat we have in the house. Those are our last chickens. Over my dead body you'll take them.'"

"In the meantime, the soldier had crawled up on the old sway-backed mare. Not only was he taking the last food the women had, but he was also going to steal the only animal they had to farm with."

"From under her long apron, Grandma Martin pulled an old double-barrel, muzzle-loading shotgun. It was loaded with dried peas and sand, but the soldier didn't know that. He didn't know the women had no ammunition. The soldier said something like, 'You won't use that gun.' She replied, 'You believe that?' And she pulled both hammers back and pelted him right in the backside. When she did, he fell off the other side of the horse, turned the chickens loose and dropped the ham. But Grandma got more than she bargained for. The soldier was so cut up from the sand and the dried peas that she had to nurse him back to health."

"'Sometimes it pays the difference to have the difference,' Grandma Martin would say when the story was told in years to come."

Granddad once gave me a big wad of Confederate money, and I treasured that all my life until Rachel's brother traded it for a pack of cigarettes long after we were married. That money and the gold-plated pistol, which I still have today, have always made me wonder what kind of good life the Harpers must have had before the war.

MAMA'S SIDE OF THE FAMILY

Mama's name was Willie Hicks Plummer. She was from a large family, and her daddy had fought through three or four different wars. He had come to America from Germany, as a stowaway on a ship when he was twelve years old. During the Civil War he lost all of his fingers on his left hand except his little finger and thumb; and on his right he only had his first two fingers and his thumb. He made a living like that until his children were old enough to farm. And then they farmed, and he fished.

Grandpa Plummer never talked much to anybody about his life back in Germany, but he did tell a close friend later on in life that his people were wealthy. Well, one day Grandpa Plummer got a letter from Germany. Nobody knows what was in that letter except that it requested that he come back to Germany. He refused. In the mean-time, Grandpa Plummer's good friend went to Germany, against my grandfather's will. And when the friend came back, he was an entirely different man, financially. So, it was generally believed by Mama and others that this friend got what could have been my grandfather's. Maybe an estate or even a castle somewhere. That is just guess work, though, because nobody knew anything more about it.

Mama and Papa got married in the middle of the road in a buggy. It was during the early farming season, cottonchopping time. Papa had got acquainted with Mama, and it was a quick courtship. About the second trip over to her house, he asked her to marry him. And they got married that same day. They were on their way to the preacher's when they met him coming toward their house in his buggy. So he performed the ceremony right there in the middle of the road—the preacher in his buggy, Papa and Mama in theirs. Then they got Mama's clothes and went on home. Mama started cooking, and Papa went to the field.

After Papa and Mama got married, Papa started branching out. He went from a three-horse farm to a five. That meant buying another two mules and maybe another 150 acres. That's how we came to have two farms, Granddad's and Papa's. (Granddad had come home after the Civil War with a couple of horses and started from there, working the land the womenfolk had saved. Rumor had it that Granddad, Papa, and

Papa's four brothers had had to fight to save the land from the carpetbaggers who started coming through after the war, cheating and swindling all they possibly could. Hints of beatings and hangings floated around all during my childhood. I always thought that my granddad, papa, and uncles took some part in these activities.) Granddad and Papa worked the two farms together for years, until Granddad couldn't go to the field.

It was 1917, and times were good.

Georgia ranked second only to Texas among the cotton-producing states. The price for cotton had been going up, reflecting war-time prosperity. In 1917, a cotton crop was worth three times what it had been worth in 1910. There also was an enormous expansion of agricultural education. The Georgia State College of Agriculture had been established in 1906 in Athens, and in that same year an agricultural and mechanical school was founded in every congressional district of the state. Two experiment stations had been set up to foster breakthroughs in Georgia farming. One of these experiment stations was just fifteen miles from the Harper farm. Frank Harper and the other farmers in the community were often visited by someone from the experiment station who made suggestions about improving the yield of the crops. Things were so good in Georgia in the years 1914–1918 that farmers were said to be suffering from "an embarrassment of riches." "It was a curious sight," one report said, "to see farmers come to town with their pockets stuffed with money." While you couldn't say the Harper family was suffering from an embarrassment of riches, they did have more cash than at any time since before the Civil War. One day Frank Harper came home with a surprise—a Whippet Overland Touring Car, one of the first automobiles to be owned by anyone in the Brooks community. What a day!

PAPA BUYS A CAR

One of the happiest days of my life was when we got our first car. I was nine years old. One Saturday morning in early spring after the cotton was sold, Papa said at breakfast, "I'm going to ride into town with Emmett Hardy this morning." Mama replied, "You're not taking your own buggy? You'll have to stay in Griffin till Emmett's ready to come home." "I have plenty to do," Papa replied. "You boys shuck corn for the hogs while I'm gone. And stay close to the house. Your mama might need you."

Nonie, Dave, and I went out to the corncrib and started shucking corn, throwing the ears into one of the half-bushel baskets Granddad had made. It was warm enough to sit on the doorsill of the corncrib and put the basket outside. We were chewing our tobacco and pulling the shucks off the corn. Not long before dinner time, we heard a noise. It was coming from the direction of the road. We jumped up to see what it was. There pulling into the yard was Papa. He was driving a car!

Everybody came running. Mama's hands were wet because she was mopping and didn't even take time to dry them. Granddad came from behind the well shelter. We couldn't believe our eyes! Papa had bought a car, and he couldn't even drive! "How'd you learn to drive that thing?" Granddad asked. "I learned to drive by driving it home," Papa replied.

Oh, it was a beautiful car. Shiny black with a windshield and a hard top. The sides were open, and there were curtains you could pull if the wind got too strong. The car had one big door on each side. And the most wonderful thing was that it would hold the whole family!

Papa said, "Everybody get in. We'll drive across Harper Mountain and back." It was the happiest moment of my life! I thought we were rich. We were people who had plenty—money in the bank and now a car! We drove across the mountain, the wind whipping in our faces. I was hanging over the side, sticking my head out so I could see around Papa. I wanted to see where we were going. That car went so much faster than the buggy! And it made such a noise. I loved it.

When we got back home, Papa said, "Now, we're just going to use this car for special occasions. We'll use the buggy the rest of the time." So, we'd get in the car on Sundays and go visit somebody. Once we went all the way to Cordele to visit Uncle Mac, Mama's brother. And another time we drove a long way—to Waco, Georgia— to see Aunt Onie, Mama's sister.

Papa would also go off in the car on drinking parties. Once he and Handy Goodin got drunk over at Digby, and Papa made a bet. "Handy, I bet my Willis Whippet will go faster backward than your Ford will go forward." Handy took him up on the bet. So they started the race, Papa driving in reverse and Handy in forward gear. Papa got to going so fast that he ran over a well, knocked the well curb off and everything. But he just kept giving the car the gas. He ended up straddling that well, but he won the bet!

MY MEANNESS STARTS TO SHOW

From the time I was little I enjoyed being mean to my sisters and fighting with my brother. I got worse as I got older. One day I fought Nonie all afternoon because he put a dead lizard in my pocket. I did not stop hitting him until he took the lizard out again. I pulled Nannie's pigtails so much that Mama had to stick them up through holes in her bonnet and tie them together. I would take chances with danger to aggravate and be mean to them.

On one particular occasion, Papa had bought a whole stalk of bananas. He hung them up in the back room which had no loft or ceiling. He just hung them up on the joists. He had to get up on a chair to cut the bananas down.

Well, here was Papa up in the chair cutting bananas for all four of us. Each one would get a banana a piece. I was first in line. Papa reached up with his knife, cut a banana off the stalk, and then handed it behind his back to the kid who was waiting next in line.

He cut the first banana and handed it back. I took the banana, peeled it, and ate it right on the spot. Papa cut the second and handed it down behind his back. I took that one, too, peeled it, and ate it on the spot. Papa cut the third banana off the stalk, handed it behind him; and I took that one, peeled it, and ate it on the spot. When Papa cut the fourth banana and handed it back, he started to get down out of the chair. The other kids said, "But, Papa, we didn't get any." "What do you mean? I handed four bananas down." "Yea, but Tom took all of them."

By that time, I was almost out of the house. Papa got back up in the chair and cut a banana for Nonie, Blanche, and Nannie. And when I ate my next banana, I took just one and remembered the whipping I got the last time. Papa was very cautious from then on when he handed bananas down.

I also didn't win any friends the time I messed with Mama's new sewing machine. Mama had been saving butter and egg money for a long time, hoping to get enough to buy a sewing machine. (She made all our clothes by hand.) This year cotton had sold for fifty cents a pound! So, Mama picked cotton hard and took some of the money she made and added it to her butter and egg money. She was finally able to buy a new White treadle sewing machine. Now she had her heart's desire, and she was making clothes for Christmas.

It was winter. The weather was cold, and it was sleeting hard. Mama had her machine set up near the fire in the big room. When she went in to fix dinner, I sat down at that machine and moved everything on it that would move. Naturally, when Mama came back to sew, the machine would not work.

"Tommie Harper, you're the one that messed with that sewing machine."

"No, Papa, I didn't do it."

"We didn't do it, Papa," Blanche, Nannie, and Nonie said.

"Who fooled with this sewing machine? I'll get everyone of you if you don't tell."

Everybody denied touching Mama's sewing machine.

"O. K., Blanche, you and Nannie, get in that back room. I'm going to lock you in there until somebody tells who did this."

"Nonie, you get in that room out on the porch."

"And, Tommie, I'm taking you out to the cottonshed, and you're going to tell me on the way that you messed with that sewing machine."

But I did not tell.

Papa threw me in the cottonshed and went back. I sat in that shed all afternoon, hearing the sleet hit the tin roof, freezing to death. But I was not going to tell. Along about dark, Papa came out, opened the door, and took me back to the house. He said on the way, "I know what I'm going to do. I'm going to whip all four of you, and then I know I'll get the right one." I piped right up and said, "That's the thing to do!" I figured that if all of us got a whipping, Papa would never catch up with me for doing it. It was years later, even after Rachel and I got married, that I told Papa and Mama I was the one who fooled with the machine.

In 1916 Georgia passed its first com- *pulsory school attendance law, but the law had many loopholes and enforcement remained poor for a long time. The law said that all children ages eight to fourteen had to attend school for at least four months of the year. However, if a child lived more than three miles from the nearest school, he or she could be excused from attending. A child could also be excused when farm work needed to be done.*

The school year in Fayette County was 135 days. The number of pupils in elementary grades totaled 1,804. The total number in the high school grades was 123. (Much of America maintained segregated schools at this time, so separate figures exist for children and young people attending schools for the Black people who lived in the community.) Graduation occurred at the end of the eleventh grade in Fayette County, although in the majority of counties in Georgia graduation occurred at the end of the tenth grade. Most pupils over the state did not graduate; they stopped going to school at the end of the seventh grade.

For instance, in 1915 attendance in the sixth grade in Fayette County was 195; in the seventh, 150; and in the eighth, 86. The ninth grade had only 20 pupils; the tenth grade, 12; and the eleventh grade, 5. (Enough people did stay in school long enough to give Fayette County a 77% literacy rate, much higher than many other Georgia counties where a literacy rate of 50% or 60% was not unusual.)

The average monthly salary for male and female teachers in the elementary grades in Fayette County was $40. Male high school teachers got $75 and female high school teachers, $65. There was a total of twenty-eight school houses, many of them one-room country schools such as the one Tommie and his sisters and brother attended for their elementary grades. Tommie continued in school two years longer than did many students; he did not quit school until the end of the ninth grade.

GOING TO SCHOOL

School started in late fall and went through early spring. Then school opened again in the summer after the laying in of the crops and continued till fodderpulling time.

We went to a one-room school with one teacher for all grades. I hated school, but I had to go. In the third grade, though, I was the teacher's pet. The reason I know is because she kept me in the third grade for three years! By the time I passed the third grade, I had almost grown kids for buddies. I was already mean, but this made me meaner.

Finally, they closed the one-room school house, and we had to ride the bus into Brooks. This caused a lot of trouble. We children from the one-room school were called country kids by the kids from town. They made fun of our dinner in a tin bucket and laughed even harder when we sat down to eat our syrup and biscuit with side meat. (The syrup was poured in a hole that was made when you stuck your finger into the biscuit.) In the fall and winter we had baked

From the Plow to the Pulpit

sweet potatoes. The town kids had light bread sandwiches, and they used a paper sack instead of a bucket.

To make matters worse, Nonie and I wore homemade overalls. You could tell because our overalls didn't have metal fasteners on them the way store-bought ones did. Our straps were fastened with buttons instead. For this reason, we were called "mama-made." This made me so mad I could bite a nail. So, I started fighting the first day. I fought until school took up; then I fought at recess. I fought again at dinner; and after school waiting on the bus, I'd fight again.

The principal whipped me the first day. And every few days thereafter. I probably got three or four whippings a week. The teacher tried to make me tell her why I fought so much. But I wouldn't tell. Finally, someone in the class told her that I fought because they called me mama-made. After that the whippings from the principal stopped, but I continued to fight at the drop of a hat. The boys would gang up on me while we were waiting on the bus. There would be three or four boys, but by the time I used my tin bucket on their heads, they would run. So, the tin bucket was a weapon as well as a dinner pail.

One day in the spring several of us from the country decided to walk home from school. I was going along the road, cursing our teacher up a storm because she had accused me of something that day that I hadn't done. Suddenly, we heard a buggy behind us—and there was the teacher. I was sure she had heard me, so I was scared to death all the rest of the way home.

Sure enough, when we got to where we could see the house, there was the teacher's buggy parked out in front. I thought to myself, "I'll just run away from home." But a few steps farther, I decided home was better and it would be easier to take a whipping; so I went on up toward the house. I found out when I got there that the teacher was talking to Mama about baking her a fruitcake for Christmas. From then on I liked school a little better and was real careful in what I said.

If I had a hard spelling test, I'd get sick. Now, you have to know I was between a brick and a hard place. Because if you stayed home, Mama gave you medicine—big Calumel tablets. We had a rain barrel outside the kitchen, so I would go out there to take this medicine. Instead of swallowing it, I'd throw the tablet into the rain barrel. I'd lie around until long about dinner time.

Then, suddenly, I'd get to feeling better and would call my dogs and head off to the woods for the rest of the day.

My school days were something to think about. I was always glad when time came to start farming. I had more fun plowing a pair of young mules than fighting a bunch of town dudes.

It was the fall of 1918. World War I *was reaching its peak; the majority of American casualties occurred during this year. Death also came from another quarter. Between mid-September and mid-November, the entire country was swept by a severe epidemic of Spanish influenza. Particularly hard hit were army camps all over the nation. Camp Gordon near Atlanta was struck violently. Deaths were a daily occurrence; at times coffins were stacked like fire wood, awaiting shipment to towns in Georgia, Alabama, and Tennessee. Visiting was confined to close relatives and required special passes. Gauze masks became standard equipment. The civilian population was also hard hit. During the first week of October, public gathering places were ordered closed—theaters, libraries, dance halls, churches. In the United States 548,000 people died from the flu; twenty million died worldwide.*

The flu epidemic hit the Brooks community hard. Many families buried two, three, or even four of their family members. The Harpers did not get through the epidemic without a death occurring in their home. Tommie's brother, J. D., eighteen months old, died from the flu. It was a traumatic time that took its toll.

WHAT IT WAS LIKE DURING THE FLU

During this time there were sickness and death in just about every home. In some homes every member of the family was sick. In many families there would be two or three deaths in one week. Young and old died alike; sometimes babies would be buried with their mothers.

Those who were able to be up went from house to house to help with the sick and take care of the stock. The men dug graves over the community all day. You could never leave a grave open at night. If you did leave a grave open at night, bad luck would come to the family. So the grave had to be closed the day it was dug. This meant that on some days there were funerals held as late as six o'clock. In some instances, a fellow helped bury the dead today and before the week was out his funeral would also be conducted.

In our family everybody was sick except Mama and me. While Mama tried to take care of the sick, my job was to take care of the outside work, the milking, feeding, watering, and cutting wood for the fireplace. Mama always said she and I didn't have time to get sick; we had too much to do.

Death came to our house as it did to others. J. D., the baby in the family, died. Since Papa was sick, some men in the community dug J.D.'s grave. The ground was frozen, which made the digging of the grave difficult. But it had to be dug. They put the coffin in a neighbor's car and took it to the grave. It was a cold and rainy day.

AFRAID TO HEAR THE BIBLE READ

Papa drank a lot, and he was rough. Every day in the field he would drink sixteen ounces of the corn liquor he made in the woods out by the side of the house—in two gulps. One in the morning and one in the afternoon. His drinking didn't affect his work, but it affected his attitude. Everybody knew you did not cross Frank Harper.

It was a custom in the community that when somebody got in trouble, all the men gathered together until the trouble was all settled. Frank Harper was usually the leader of this group. These would always be times of great danger, and sometimes somebody would be killed or hurt real bad before the night was over. When Papa left home to go settle some trouble, Mama started to pray.

Now, when I was a little boy, there was no claim made that the Harper family was religious. Nobody went to church, except the first week in August when my sisters attended the community protracted meeting. Mama was religiously inclined, but Papa wasn't. As a rule, we didn't read the Bible in the house. So you could say we were not religious.

But when Papa would leave to go meet the other men, Mama would get the old family Bible down. She'd gather us kids around her in front of the fire, and she'd read. Something about the coming of the Lord. Of course, none of us could understand what she was reading, but I was very disturbed with the thought of dying and staying dead so long. She read about some of the dead coming up and some not. I never could figure out how a person could stay dead so long. And that would scare the life out of me to just think about how long you'd have to stay dead. It always made a deep impression in my mind. This little boy would get as close to his Mama as I could when she was reading the Bible, afraid to move.

Then when Mama began to pray, this was just about more than I could take. But after a few days without the Bible reading, I would forget about dying or staying dead so long and get back in the old ways. I was mean to my sisters, fought with my brother, and would curse any one that fussed with me, taking chances with danger just to prove my point.

While they were enjoying the bonanza
years of 1910–1918, Georgia farmers had no idea what lay ahead. What the Harpers and thousands of other farmers did not know was that the boll weevil, which had entered Georgia in 1913, would soon destroy them. The boll weevil caused a three percent loss to Georgia cotton crops in 1916; the loss rose to ten percent by 1918. But the U. S. Department of Agriculture had made a remarkable discovery of an effective weevil control, calcium arsenate, so farmers were dusting their cotton with that, completely reassured that all would be well. But by 1919, Tommie's eleventh year, it was clear that neither calcium arsenate nor anything else was going to stop the boll weevil from destroying the crop. For the next five years,

until 1924, when Tommie was sixteen, farmers were plagued by the boll weevil. Yield dropped from 200 pounds an acre to eighty pounds an acre all over Georgia. The state's total cotton crop dropped from two million bales in 1918 to 558,000 in 1923 and would never be the same again. (Georgia farmers were going to be in almost constant economic distress until 1933, when Tommie was twenty-five years old.) Farmers lost. Merchants lost. Bankers lost. Everybody lost. The "winged demon" caused panic and disaster.

THE YEAR THAT PAPA WENT BROKE

After the boll weevil struck and times got dark, Papa almost murdered a man over our Willis Whippet Overland Touring Car.

It happened like this:

The first year the boll weevil hit our crop, instead of thirty to thirty-five bales, we made ten bales of cotton to six plows. The next year was even worse. Nothing was made, and the farm was in debt. We couldn't pay our taxes, and we couldn't pay the bank. Many farmers were forced to leave the community and try to seek work in town. We lived with our backs to the wall, staying on the farm, working hard, living close, and doing without a lot of things.

To stay ahead of the boll weevil, farmers had been advised to fertilize high and grow the cotton fast. But this was a great mistake, as the boll weevil loved the shade of the large cotton plants. In just two years of this kind of farming, we lost everything.

The second year Papa bought a young mule from a dealer in Brooks, as it was necessary to get at least one new mule every year. But no cotton was made this year, so there was no money to pay the debt. The bank gave us a year longer to come up with the money we had borrowed from them, and this brought hope to our family.

But the stock dealer at Brooks, who had a mean reputation for charging exorbitant interest and who many people said was a crook, wouldn't give us a year longer to pay for the mule. He demanded full payment now.

Finally, he came out to the house to get his money. Mama and the girls were up on the porch, and Papa and the rest of us were standing out in the yard. Papa said to the stock dealer, "Buck, I don't have any money to pay you. Can you give me till next year?" Buck looked around the yard and out toward the barn. It was clear his answer was no. "I'll just take the mule back, then, and I'll take your car. You'll still owe me money." Papa's face swelled up, and his lips trembled. "Buck, there's nothing left for you to take," he said.

"Well, I'll just take those four milk cows out in the cow lot." (A young mule sold for $175, and cows brought $25 or $30 a piece. Papa owed for the mule plus the high interest the dealer had been charging him all year.)

The dealer said to his helper, "Lead those cows out of the cow lot." Papa got madder than he already was. He lost his temper and whipped his pistol out of his pocket. The helper looked at Papa and then he replied, "No, Mr. Buck, I can't lead those cows out of the cow lot, for I'm not ready to die." The dealer was furious. "Well," he said, "I'll just do it myself."

Papa said, "If you open that gate, you'll die." And he started walking toward the dealer. Buck knew he was about to die, so he began to beg Papa not to kill him. Papa then ordered him off the place. "You've got five minutes to get that car and get off this place, or I'll kill you for sure." And Papa would have. The dealer went running toward our car, jumped in, and tried to start it. But the motor was dead. He then jumped out of the car, pushed it out of the yard onto the road, left it there, and went running down the road. He had somebody else come out later and get the car.

Things got so bad that the bank closed in Brooks. Granddad had a little money saved in the bank. When he heard about the closing, he walked two and a half miles, mad as an old wet hen. (He was Irish with a high temper.)

Well, he walked up to the bank door, and it was locked. He knocked on the door with his walking stick. A man came to the door and said, "You can't come in; the bank is closed." Granddad knocked the fellow down with his stick, walked into the bank, stayed a while, and walked out. He never spoke to a person outside. He just walked straight on back home. When asked about his money later, he'd say, "Some lost all they had; some didn't."

At Christmas that year there was no cash to buy any presents, for children or grownups alike. Times were hard, and hearts were heavy. Then, on Christmas day . . .

THE MIRACLE OF THE CHRISTMAS CALF

My warmest memory from child-hood is the morning we found the miracle calf.

It was Christmas time. We never had a Christmas tree, so Mama and Papa put out card-board boxes by the fireplace to hold what Santa Claus brought us kids. This was usually oranges and apples, some hard candy and nuts, a pair of overalls or a dress (made by Mama) and in a good year a pair of shoes and some socks. This year, though, had been a terrible year. The cotton crop had failed, so there was no money to buy anything.

On Christmas Eve, Nonie, my sisters and I had all gathered in one corner of the house to discuss what we thought we would get for Christmas. "We're not going to get anything," Nonie said, and I quickly agreed with him. "You know Papa doesn't have any money." But my sisters insisted that Santa Claus would still come and bring us gifts. Nonie and I were pretty easily con-vinced, because we wanted some presents so much. "But how can Santa Claus get down the chimney with such a big fire in the fireplace?" we all puzzled. "He's sure to get burned." We spent the rest of the evening discussing this terrible dilemma, suggesting first one thing and another that we thought might work.

When we got up on Christmas morning, though, our boxes held only some apples from the orchard and some pecans from the trees out in the yard. We had worried and figured out the problem of the hot chimney for nothing. Santa Claus hadn't even come.

There was a turkey cooking in a washtub on top of the cookstove, though, and that was something unusual. We had never had a turkey for Christmas before. Mama had decided to raise turkeys that fall to help make ends meet, but then nobody had the money to buy the turkeys when Papa took them to Griffin to be sold at Bass's Mercantile Store. That's why we were able to have a turkey for Christmas. It was the only special thing about the day.

After Nonie and I looked in our boxes, we headed down to the cow lot to milk the cows. Our spirits were about as low as they could get.

When we went in to the shed, Nonie said, "Tom, look! A baby calf! A baby calf got born last night."

"Let's go tell Papa," I said.

We ran as fast as we could, got Papa, and ran back to the cow lot.

Papa went into the shed. He picked up the calf. "Hey, boys," he said. "Come look."

We crowded closer and looked at the calf. We could hardly believe what we saw. Right there, in the middle of that little calf's forehead, was a big white star. "This is going to be a Christmas present for your Mama," Papa said. "Let's go give it to her right now."

Can you see this big, 240 pound, 6'3" man going up the path with a tiny baby calf in his arms, two small boys running along behind him? We were calling, "Mama. Mama. Come see what Santa Claus brought you."

Papa set the baby calf down on the back porch and called out, "Willie, come out and receive your Christmas present."

When Mama saw that little calf with the white star on his forehead, she cried. And then she hugged Papa! She hugged Nonie and me! "I'm going to name this little calf Christmas Star," Mama said. "This cow is never going to be sold, and she's never going to be killed. She's a part of the Harper family forever."

This was a present that lasted a long, long time. The calf made a very good milk cow, and we kept her until she died of old age.

WE GET BACK ON OUR FEET

We managed to pay our debt on the farm the next year by working on the roads with the CC camps. We would get paid two dollars a day for taking our team and wagon and helping to level bridges and repair the roads. Mama made ends meet by picking wild mustard, pepper grass, and polk salad to feed the family until the garden came in. We had no meat. We did make syrup from our sugar cane, and we had bread made from the Red Dog Shorts we used to feed the hogs. Many meals during this time consisted of butter, syrup, and bread.

There was no money to get fertilizer to make the next crop, so we mixed our own fertilizer with whatever we could get. We managed to have enough fertilizer for fifteen of our 260 acres. Then Papa traded with Mr. Mask, a big farmer in the community, to work twenty acres for halves. To make ends meet, we also started selling wood to the mill villagers in town who used it in their cookstoves.

When cottonpicking time came, we picked the cotton on Mr. Mask's place first. We made nineteen bales on the twenty acres. Mr. Mask gave Papa ten bales and he took nine. Then on our own farm, we made twelve bales on the fifteen acres we had been able to plant. That year the cotton sold for twenty to thirty cents a pound, and this helped us get on our feet again. We would pick cotton all day, go home, feed the stock, milk the cows, eat supper, take two oil lanterns, go to the woods, cut two loads of wood, load the wagon, and be ready to set out for town to deliver the wood by daylight the next morning.

Hauling wood during these years was done summer and winter. Several of the neighbors came to depend on Papa to do their shopping while he was in town delivering the wood. Coming home, we'd stop at each house and give them their order. And it would be dark when we got home. Mama would have a good, hot supper waiting. We would then tell all we learned that day. Some of the time we would have a mess of mullet fish for breakfast on Sunday.

MY FIRST RABBIT WITH A GUN

I was twelve years old. We were picking cotton on a crisp fall Saturday morning. There were eight or nine of us in the field. We were working hard to finish up before the cold weather started. Papa had gone to Griffin on some business, leaving us to work in the field until he got back. Roy, Sweet Charity's boy, was field boss. Now this man was a worker, and he wanted to please Mr. Frank. And did. Nobody played around with Roy. I mean, you had to work.

Well, I had a pack of good dogs, even though at twelve years of age I wasn't considered old enough to hunt. Papa brought me my first pup a few years before when he came back from a coon hunt with a fellow named Padgett. He was a little scrubby-looking dog, but I loved him. I named that little pup Tiger, and from then on I collected as many hunting dogs as I could get. I took care of the dogs, and Papa and the others hunted them. I was just waiting until I was big enough to hunt.

All my dogs had names. You didn't call them just dogs. You called them Spot, Bill, Old

Gray Boy, Sam, Rock, Tig, Trail Blazer. Each dog knew his or her place at feeding time. (Mama would make big pans of corn bread to feed the dogs. Sometimes she'd have to fire up the stove just to cook bread for these dogs, and she'd be aggravated about that until the hunters brought in the rabbits and the squirrels.)

My dogs always went to the field with us and would run rabbits all day. And if they ever cornered a rabbit, I went to them. This would make Papa so mad he couldn't stand it. "Tom Harper, I'll be glad when you're grown enough to take care of yourself. You'll starve. Because you're not worth the salt in your bread, always running off after those dogs when you ought to stay in the field."

Well, the dogs had a rabbit going this Saturday morning and Papa was gone. I guess I thought I'd slip by Roy. In just a little while, I got to the end of the row, hung my sack on a stalk of cotton, and away I went up to the house. I was headed to get Papa's gun, something nobody was allowed to do. Especially a twelve-year-old boy who had never shot anything except a pistol, which Papa let me shoot one Sunday afternoon when I was six.

But today I was going to get myself a rabbit. I got Papa's old single-barrel shotgun out of the rack. It was easy for me to slip out with the gun because Saturday was a busy day for Mama. It was the day when she did all the ironing and scrubbed the floors with a corn-shuck mop.

I went back to the field and hid the gun in my cotton sack. The dogs were running in the swamp across from the field. As I got out to the end of the row near the woods, I slipped the gun out of my cotton sack and headed down toward the swamp. The rabbit came out of the woods and sat down in a clear place, not far from the cotton field. I raised the gun up and pulled the trigger. The gun went one way, and I went the other. Of course, everybody in the field heard the gun and then saw me falling back on the ground from the blast. Old Roy came running down to where I was. He kept asking, "You all right? You all right?"

The shells were New Club, old black-powder shells. You'd shoot, and then you'd have to fan smoke out of your eyes to see whether you'd killed anything or not. When I got up off the ground and managed to wave the smoke out of my eyes, I found the rabbit. I had not only killed it; I had shot it to pieces. But I was so proud. I headed up to the house as fast as I could. Tears of joy were streaming down my face. I had killed my first rabbit. I was taking that rabbit to show Mama!

But I didn't bargain on Roy getting up to the house first and telling Mama what had happened. She, of course, gave me a switching for slipping the gun out, and she also added, "Your Papa will take care of you when he gets home." Roy said, "I know he will, Miss Willie, because I'm gonna tell him!"

Well, that just about took all the fun out of my first rabbit hunt. But, as it happened, the dogs caught another rabbit that afternoon in a hollow tree. I left the field again to get the rabbit. That gave us two rabbits for supper.

Roy didn't see Papa when he came back from town, so Papa didn't know anything yet about the gun. We got all the feeding and milking done and went in for supper. I was scared to death the whole time. When we sat down to eat, there on the table was a big dish of fried rabbit with sweet milk gravy and hot biscuits. Papa said, "Willie, where did you get the rabbits?" There was a long quiet spell. Then Mama answered, "Tom shot them." This started a serious talk about the gun and a promise of a tanning with the rawhide buggy whip, which I knew I would get, for Papa always kept his promises.

Then there was a talk between Granddad and Papa. Yes, they decided, I could start hunting now. I could use Granddad's gun so long as I hunted by myself. That brought to life the hunter for the family. From that time on, and as long as I was home, I brought in the family's meat.

I WANTED TO BE LIKE PAPA

All my life, from the time I was little, if you asked me what I wanted to be when I grew up, I'd say, "I want to be like my Papa." I had learned to shoot a pistol almost as well as he could. I had learned how to do everything on the farm. I tried to be what he was, and what he could do I wanted to do better.

And that included, I guess, being mean.

Because the older I got, the more I started taking after my dad. I fought at the drop of a hat. I never saw a man I was afraid of, and I would take on three or four boys at a time. I started carrying a pistol when I was thirteen, and I carried it everywhere I went. I never used it to kill or hit anyone, but it was not my goodness that kept me from it.

There was a time when we were swimming in Flint River. We'd had to wait for a baptizing to be over; and we stayed on the bank an extra hour before going in, after the church people left. We wanted to be sure their sins had washed on down the river. When we put our clothes back on after swimming and were ready to leave, a gang of boys on the other bank hollered at us.

The Moon brothers lived nearby; and since our farm was two miles or more down the road, they said we were intruding on their territory. "Don't you ever come back here swimming again. This is our part of the river," one of the Moon boys said. This order led to some sharp words. "Come over here, and we'll show you whose part of the river this is," we yelled back.

One of the boys jumped off the bank and swam across the river to where we were. He pulled a knife on me. My pistol was on him before he knew what was happening. A friend grabbed the gun; the hammer fell on his thumb and first finger, causing the gun not to fire. All the boys then ran, and there was never any more trouble about the swimming hole. And I'd been saved from shooting a man by a friend's thumb on the hammer of my gun.

The next time I almost killed a man was at a country store. Nonie and I were walking up to the store when a friend of ours pulled up in an old truck. He had a dead snake about five feet long, but we didn't know it was dead. Knowing that I was frightfully scared of snakes, the boy started to throw the dead snake on me. I pulled my gun on him before he knew what had happened. Nonie knocked the gun out of my hand, and the bullet cut the band off the fellow's hat. That ended the snake throwing. The fellow was, of course, frightened and said, "Never had a man come so close to death because of a dead snake."

THIS ONE WILL BE YOUR PREACHER BOY

I t was the first week of August, time for the protracted meeting at the County Line Christian Church. Blanche and Nannie went to this meeting every year. There was church every morning and every night. And between these services, the young people would all go home with somebody to eat dinner and to visit in the afternoon. The preacher was also invited to join the crowd.

On this particular day, everybody, including the preacher, came home with Blanche and Nannie. I had no warning that they were coming, so I didn't have time to slip off down to the river, which I always did if I knew people were coming to the house. I was real bashful and shy.

So they caught me at home this time.

As was the custom, the older folks ate dinner first, and the children waited for the second table. When we did sit down to eat, I was as nervous as a thirteen-year-old could be. Brother Goodson, the preacher, came into the kitchen while we were eating. He started teasing me about the girls. This made matters even worse.

Because one thing I couldn't stand was girls. When Papa would hire Nonie and me out to one of our neighbors at planting time, I would be so nervous at dinner. When the red-haired daughter of the family brought a glass of milk to set down at my place, I'd knock the milk over as soon as she sat it down. Then I couldn't eat very much because I was so embarrassed. I would be so hungry by the time I got home that I could eat a cow. This would happen day after day, for a week or two weeks. I thought it ought to be against the law to hire boys out, especially if there were girls in the family that waited on tables and carried water to the field for the thirsty plowboys. The water would spill out of the dipper before you could even drink.

So, the preacher was standing in the kitchen teasing me about the girls. Then something very strange happened. Reverend Goodson suddenly stopped talking, almost in mid-sentence. You could have heard a pin drop. Without saying another word, he walked over, stood behind me at the table, put his hand on my head, and said to Mama, "Miss Willie, this one will be your preacher boy."

Everybody in the kitchen just looked and stared. Somebody snickered. Something must be wrong with this preacher; he certainly doesn't know who he is talking about, that's for sure. When Reverend Goodson left the room, everybody laughed; and one of the girls said, "Well, he's sure got you mixed up with somebody else, Tom Harper."

And from the looks of things that itinerant preacher, a stranger in our midst, couldn't have been more wrong. Many years of mean and dangerous living were still ahead. But he must have known something that the rest of us didn't know because his prophecy did come true.

It was 1922; Tommie was fourteen

*years old. Even though the worst of the boll weevil dev-
astation was past—entire crops were no longer being de-
stroyed—cotton yield was never again to be what it was
during the bonanza years of 1910–1918. Cotton prices in
Georgia had fallen from thirty-six cents per pound in
1919 to seventeen cents per pound in 1922. For the years
1920–1924, the average yield per acre in Georgia was
133 pounds, the lowest recorded since the 1870s. In
Fayette County it was not unusual for yield to be as low
as eighty or ninety pounds per acre; in the past the
farmers had been used to getting as much as 200.*

*While the Harpers had recovered from the devas-
tation of whole years without making anything, they
were still in a serious economic bind. They could not
make their living on farming alone. This made the woodcutting and selling they had begun in 1919 essential to
their livelihood. Fortunately, Georgia had more trees
than any other state in the Union; and in the 215 square
miles of Fayette county alone there were 25,000 acres of
forest—pine, oak, hickory, gum, poplar, walnut, maple,
and chestnut. The Harper farm had its share of these
trees. It was from these woods that the men cut the
stovewood which they sold in town.*

*Ice storms were not unusual during the hard
winter months, but the ice storm of 1922 was the most
severe in anyone's memory. The storm lasted for two
weeks. Frank Harper had to drive nails into his shoes
and then cut the heads off to make spikes so he could
walk outside without slipping down. Birds of all kinds
came to the barn for shelter from the cold. Some of the
cattle froze in the barn. The three fireplaces in the Harper
farmhouse were kept going night and day. The water in
the number ten quart bucket froze solid during the day.
At night there would be so many covers on the bed that
the sleepers could hardly turn over. The next morning*

when they woke up there was ice on the covers where they had breathed during the night. Tommie was caught out in the elements the day the storm began.

THE ICE STORM

Times were hard. The only way we could make ends meet was to cut wood and take it into town to sell to the mill villagers for their cookstoves.

Woodcutting time had always been as regular as winter. When it started getting cold, every able-bodied man on the place was put in the woods. There had to be 100 cords of stovewood cut and stacked for Mama's use in the kitchen. We would cut the wood for the fireplaces as we needed it. Now we had to cut a lot more, enough to take at least one wagonload into town each week.

The woodcutting was done like this: two men with a cross cut saw would cut the trees. Two men would split the log, and one would stack the wood in cords. A cord would be four feet wide, eight feet long, and four feet high. To see 100 cords stacked in the woods was a beautiful sight. Each cord was raked around so if the woods burned, the fire would not get to the wood that was stacked. (To set fire to a man's woods was almost like stealing his horse. It was a good way to be hung or whipped with a bullwhip. So there were not very many woods burned off.)

Two men in good timber could cut five to six cords of wood in a day if they kept their saw sharp. (The saw was sharpened in the morning and then again at dinner time.) The men splitting the wood could not split and stack five or six cords of wood in a day, so the ones cutting would stop cutting and help the splitters catch up.

When you were cutting wood, you could stay warm everywhere but your feet. So we would build a fire. When our feet got so cold that we could hardly stand it, we would stop long enough to get them warm; then we'd go back to work. Before we started taking wood into town to sell, woodcutting for the winter lasted about a month. If we had very much bad weather, woodcutting could last two months and longer.

This year, with times being so hard, we started cutting wood every night after we worked in the field during the day. And we cut summer and winter. We would sell a wagonload of wood for three dollars, one dollar on delivery and a dollar a week until paid for. By this time, we had a regular route and we knew all our customers by name. The mill villagers depended on us for their wood, and we depended on selling the wood for our survival. So there wasn't anything during this time much more important than getting the wood into town.

We would usually deliver the wood on Saturday. But if we had enough customers that week, we might take a wagonload in during the week. This was true the first time Papa ever let me drive the wagon into town by myself to sell the wood. I was fourteen.

On Thursday night after we cut the wood and got it up to the house, Papa said, "Tom, you're going to drive the wagon into town tomorrow." My heart swelled with pride.

When we got up on Friday morning, it was cold. The wind was blowing out of the east, and the sky was overcast with dark clouds that threatened rain any minute. When I got ready to leave for town, Granddad brought out his heavy overcoat. "Tom, take this with you. This weather is liable to get worse before it gets better." Driving a young pair of mules, I started the fifteen miles to Griffin with the wood.

Just a few miles from the house, the cold rain started. And a few miles farther down the road, the rain started freezing on my clothes. I put on the overcoat, and in just another few miles the coat was covered with ice. I drove the mules hard. Solid ice tags were hanging from the bridles and leather driving lines.

I knew the danger the mules and I were in. During the cold and bad weather, we always had to bring the cattle in. They would go to the thick woods and stay where lots of brush protected them from the snow, sleet, and cold rain. We used dogs to drive them out of the brush. The cattle then were roped and driven to the barn where they could be fed. Sometimes during an ice storm the cattle would freeze to death. There was always a chance that some old bull would not be caught and would be out for the worse of the winter.

I made it to Griffin and unloaded the wood. I fed the mules with them still hitched to the wagon, something that was never done. The team had to have time to rest before starting the trip back home. But not this time. The ladies in the houses where I was delivering the wood called out, "Come in and get warm before you head back to the country." But I refused. I was in a hurry to get on my way back home.

The mules were young enough for me to trot them all fifteen miles back. And this probably saved my life. I got back to the house about 4:00. My face, hands and feet were so cold that Papa and others had to carry me into the house. Papa put the mules in a warm stall. My clothes were frozen so hard that Granddad's overcoat stood up on the floor when they took it off. Mama started soaking my hands and feet in cold water, adding hot water a little at a time until life began to come back into the cold flesh. She wrapped me in a cold, wet sheet before the fire and in a little while, which seemed like hours to me and the family, I came through. I had no sickness of any kind, and there was no frostbite on my hands, feet or face.

After the ordeal was over, Papa asked me, "Son, why didn't you turn around and come back home?"

I answered, "You told me never to give up on a job."

Then Papa said, "Son, you make me proud."

For that I would have made the trip back into town again.

I ALMOST COME TO HATE GOD

We had a neighbor who had three daughters and no sons. This left him very short-handed in the field. So Papa often hired Nonie and me out to this gentleman. One year Papa had bought some shingles from this neighbor, who also owned a shingle mill. To pay off the debt, Nonie and I worked extra for the man that year during spring plowing.

I had always thought the world of this neighbor. In fact, he was the only man I knew who went to church all the time. He was a very important man in the church, so I knew he must be a very good man. I looked up to him.

On this particular day I had a lot on my mind as we worked in the field. I had just been to a dance over at the Cobb place. (I always stayed out in the yard while people danced.) Some of the boys at the dance had tormented a little dog by pouring penetrating liniment on the puppy and driving it almost to distraction. I fought these boys so hard that I finally couldn't stand up. Then I sat on the ground and kept fighting them with a piece of lead pipe. I was thinking as I plowed alongside our neighbor, "Now, here's a man who would never do anything like that."

And then something happened. We were plowing short rows. With short rows, you had to turn the mule around on other rows to start back the other way. It was almost impossible for the mule to turn around without stepping on the corn and mashing it. When this happened at the end of the first row, the man jerked the mule around, cursed it, and starting beating it. I had never heard a man talk so terrible to an animal. Most people recognized their mules as property and took care of them. And here was a man who was supposed to be a fine man of God, mistreating his mule. He was like a mad man. I had never seen anybody be so cruel to an animal.

I was so mad that I just left the field. I got on my horse and went home. I said to myself, "If this man is a Christian, I don't want any part of it." From that time on I wouldn't let anybody even speak of God in my presence. I almost hated God.

MAN ON A RAILROAD BRIDGE

One day we were in the field planting cotton. Mr. Will Lunsford suddenly appeared and started talking to Papa. Then Papa called Blanche and said, "Here, you run this planter; I've got to go to the house and get the buggy." Papa and Mr. Lunsford went up to the house and got in the buggy. They rode off as fast as they could.

There was trouble in the community. Some man had done wrong to another man's wife. When Papa and Mr. Lunsford arrived at the old Mask homeplace, the men in the community had already cornered the man they were hunting in a piece of big woods. But these were woods you could stay in for days, just going and going and doubling back.

Papa, Mr. Lunsford, and the others got hot on the wrong-doer's trail. Papa and Mr. Lunsford stationed themselves in the road so they could catch the man when he came up out of the woods. The rest of the group hunting the man were going to go into the woods from the other side.

But it didn't happen the way Papa thought it would. When the hunted man came up out of the woods, he jumped right into the middle of the road and started shooting. He didn't take any aim. He just shot. Again and again. He shot right into Mr. Lunsford's face and blew his eyes out on the spot. Will was blind for life.

When Papa came back home that day, he left the mule hitched to the buggy out in front of the house, something he never did. He started walking up toward the house. Mama knew something was wrong, so she went to meet him. Papa said, "Will Lunsford got his eyes shot out today." And then he came into the house, sat down, and cried. This was only the second time I had ever seen Papa cry. The time before was when my little brother, J. D., died during the flu epidemic.

Now, Papa was one of the best pistol shots you would ever see. And nobody ever said later that he killed that hunted man. And he didn't say so either. All that anyone ever got out of him was, "The last time I saw him he was on the Chestlehurst railroad trestle over Lion Creek." But by that everybody knew.

From that time on, Papa was never the same. He stopped being the ringleader in the community. He stayed home at night. But he also was sick a lot, and he drank even more than before.

A REPUTATION GROWS

It was a custom in our community that everybody got together and hunted the day before Thanksgiving. We hunted to kill the rabbits needed for the stew the women would cook the next day. I had some of the best hunting dogs in the community, so my dogs were always used.

It was Thanksgiving day of 1923; I was fifteen. The dogs had been run hard on the rabbit hunt the day before, so I was giving them the day off. But Nonie stole the dogs out to take them hunting with a crowd of boys from Atlanta. I heard my dogs running down on the river. And I knew what had happened. With fire in my eyes, I left the men sitting around in the backyard, went down to the river, and got my dogs.

Of course, this caused bad feelings between me and the group that was hunting. There was a threatened fight. They tried to make me leave the dogs in the woods with them. But the boys soon learned that I meant business. They finally went back to hunting, but without my dogs. The air was thick with threats and hate.

That night one of the boys from the group

showed up in our yard. He had come to kill me. When Nonie told me that somebody wanted me out in the yard, I went out there. This fellow was leaning against a buggy with a double-barrel shotgun and a 45 caliber pistol.

Now I had done something that night that I never did: I had taken my pistol off and left it in the bedroom. Of course, the first thing I did when I saw the fellow with the shotgun and the pistol was to go for my gun. When I realized I didn't have it, I began to curse the fellow and push the wheel of the buggy. This knocked the man off balance and caused him to drop his guns.

About this time an old man who worked for the fellow's family came to take him home. I accused the old man of bringing the guy to the house to kill me, but he denied it. I said, "If I ever find out that you did bring him here, I will kill you."

Three days later the old man was found dead in a pine thicket. All the blame pointed to the one who had said, "If I ever find out . . . , I will kill you." I held out that I had not even seen the old man since that Thanksgiving night.

The coroner made his findings known a few days later. The old man had frozen to death. There was not a mark on him. So, my name in that incident was cleared. But my reputation in the community as a rough and mean young man increased. I was known as somebody who did what he had to do and told you why later. I rode my black bay horse, the one Mr. Emmett Hardy gave me, packed my pistol, and stayed away from all the girls.

PAPA STOPS DRINKING

I always thought I might have had something to do with Papa stopping drinking. After the incident when Will Lunsford's eyes got shot out, Papa was never the same. He drank a lot.

One day I heard the doctor tell Papa that if he didn't quit drinking and didn't quit taking so many Calumel tablets for his stomach that he would die. This frightened me so much that all I could think of night and day was, "What will make Papa stop drinking?" I didn't want him to die. I finally got up the courage to do something that might help the situation—but it also could have got me killed.

Now, Papa hated cards. He hated cards worse than anything in the world. Gambling was something he could not abide. I had heard the old superstition for a long time that if you took a deck of cards and put them on the kitchen table, somebody in the house would stop drinking. I finally got desperate enough to try it, even though Papa had threatened to kill anybody who ever brought a deck of cards into his house.

One day I went up to a sharecropper's cabin and bought a pack of cards for a nickel. Then I took that deck of cards into our house and put it on the kitchen table. I don't know to this day how I dared to do it. It's a wonder that Frank Harper didn't kill his son. But I carried those cards in there and pitched them down on the table. I did not want Papa to die.

When he saw the deck, Papa thundered, "Who put these cards on this table?"

I spoke up and said, "I did."

"Take them out of this house," he ordered.

I defied Papa for the first time in my life.

"I want you to stop drinking. So, I'll take the cards out of the house when you quit drinking, and I won't take them out before."

Papa looked at me, and he didn't say a word. He looked down at the table, and then he looked at me. I think something snapped for him, because it wasn't too long after that, that he quit drinking.

Life on the farm had a certain kind of *circularity. Even as flu epidemics, boll weevils and ice storms impacted the Harpers' lives, there remained a sameness to the turn of a year. You were bound by nature to a schedule of planting, cultivating, and harvesting. That schedule, in turn, determined the ebb and flow of life in the community.*

THE CYCLE OF A YEAR

Winter.

New Year's Day we would spend working, but we'd have a traditional meal for good luck and abundance. There would be black-eyed peas to insure plenty of coins; and there would be col lards to insure plenty of greenbacks. By daybreak on New Year's Day we'd be up, watching the road. Hosie Lynch was sure to drive up in his buggy any minute. Hosie believed the superstition that if a woman came to your house to visit first on New Year's, you'd have terrible luck all year. So, to avoid this calamity, he made the rounds of every house in the community early every New Year's Day so that a man would have crossed the threshold before any woman could arrive. (We lived by superstitions in our community. Don't rock an empty rocker, or somebody will get sick. If an owl comes outside, heat a shovel and go out and burn the owl's feet so it will leave. If you don't, somebody will die. Don't put a hat on a bed. Don't stand a broom on the handle end. No washing on the first or last Friday of the year; it'll bring you bad luck. If hogs carried sticks in their mouths, it was soon going to be cold enough to have hog killing.)

Our work for the winter months was gathering corn and cutting wood. This didn't leave much time for anything else. But on rainy days it was hunting time!

I had become very good with a gun. Almost as soon as I started hunting at twelve, Papa let me leave the field once a week to go hunting so we could have fresh meat on the table. I'd kill a mess of squirrels, maybe eight at a time, and bring them home. We'd have fried squirrels and dumplings for a day or two. The year that I got my thumb cut off with an ax when we were chopping wood, I couldn't carry a shotgun. So for that entire year, I learned to hunt with a pistol. I could kill more rabbits with a pistol than anybody else could with a shotgun. I got so good that if a rabbit ever got out into the open, that rabbit was mine. That rabbit didn't go anywhere else.

If it had rained a lot, Flint River would flood the swamps. Then the buck rabbits had to go to higher ground. The buck rabbit was much bigger than the cottontail. If you killed eight or ten bucks, as well as cottontails, you had a heavy load to carry home. I'd often kill twelve or fifteen and have to drag them on the ground behind me. Mama and Papa would dress the rabbits and make rabbit sausage.

One night I went hunting with my dog Tig. Tig was running something in the woods. It was getting dark, and the dog was down below the house. The dog kept on running. Across the mountain. Down towards the river. With me chasing along right behind him. Finally, Tig came to a sudden stop. We got to the fork of some branches, and Tig just quit.

So I sat down on the ground and lit my pipe. All at once, in the quiet and peace of the night, a bobcat screamed out at Tig and me. Out of the swamp came the dog. Off of my head came my hat. Out of my mouth came the pipe-stem. I had bit that pipestem completely in two! That was about the funniest thing that ever happened to me hunting.

I did almost all my hunting alone. Just me and my dogs. And to be in the woods hunting in the rain! I loved that. I would walk along under the trees getting soaking wet and then come home and sit in front of the fire until my clothes dried.

S pring.

By the time hunting ended in the late winter, we started fishing with our nets. These nets were about three feet deep and six to ten feet long. We would use two poles, one short and one long enough to get the net about six or seven feet from the bank. This fishing was done in still water. We would bait our hooks with corn bread to catch red and white suckers, some of which would go four and a half or five pounds each. In a week of fishing, we would catch as much as seventy-five pounds.

In the spring when the dogwoods bloomed, it was time to start fishing with set hooks. This was also cottonplanting time, so Papa would let me off from the field work to go set out the hooks. It would take about all the afternoon to set 100 or 150 hooks. The hooks were tied to a short pole that was stuck into the bank. I would start around the Holly branch and work down the river to the old Sawmill Lake. Then I'd start back up, checking each hook to see that it was still baited. Some time I would catch fifteen or twenty catfish on the return trip. By the time I got back to where I had started from, it would be getting dark. The next morning before daybreak, we would be back taking up the hooks. On any good night of fishing, we would catch thirty-five or forty pounds of catfish on the 150 hooks. I then would go home, proud of my double string of fish, tired but ready for a long day in the field. The family would enjoy a big fish dinner with enough left over for breakfast the next morning.

We fished every weekend, but never on Sunday. If we went fishing on Saturday night, we had to quit at midnight. My Papa might be mean, but he did not let us violate the Sabbath. He never allowed us to fish or hunt on Sunday. He never gave us a reason when we pestered him. He just said, "It's not allowed."

The first thing we'd have to do in the spring, even before we started planting cotton, was to clean out the ditch banks in the bottom land where we were going to plant corn later on. We always planted seven to twelve acres of corn in the bottoms. The dirt was black and rich and would produce eighty to a hundred bushels of corn per acre. We needed the corn to feed the stock. Also the meal for the family's bread was ground from this corn. If we didn't clean out the ditch banks, the branches would flood the young corn if we should have lots of spring rain.

This was also the time for breaking a pair of young mules, which had to be done every year. Papa would buy a pair of mules that had never had a halter on them. These mules knew nothing about working in the field. They had to be broken first to the presence of the bridle bits in their mouths. Then they were put to the wagon to pull a load of compost or wood. This was a job for Nonie and me. We knew we had better not let the mules run away, which was a common thing for young mules. Lucky for us we never had this happen, even though we were just young boys when we took up this job.

S_ummer.

It was time to start breaking the land for planting the crop. Every man and boy that could work was given a job. This started the long hot days from daylight until dark, with a hour out for dinner. When you put a day in on the Harper farm, no one had to rock you to sleep at night. The mules and the men that plowed them would be ringing wet with sweat. The mules would be covered with white froth where the harness rubbed. Their sweat would look like soap suds. We took care of our mules, but we worked them hard. A field hand might say to Papa, "Mr. Frank, don't you think we ought to make these mules blow?" (That meant let them rest.) Papa would answer, "If you kill a mule, I'll buy another one." We had to get the work done. You couldn't plant cotton and corn after the time nature and the moon said to plant them.

Every mule had a name—like Tom or Jack, Nell, Bird, Maude and Blackie. Each mule had a set of harnesses that hung in a certain place on the rack on the platform of the crib. Each person who plowed these mules knew exactly where his mule's harness was. Nobody took anything off your harness and put it on his.

We'd dress up our mules' bridles—put a band across the nose and run some decoration down on the leather strip that went between their eyes. I'd save a cow's tail when we killed a beef and put a wire through the tail. Then I'd hang this tail as a decoration on the buckle of the harness where the band came over—like a tail hanging on the side of a coonskin cap. You took a personal interest in your mule, but that didn't keep you from working it hard.

After we got the cotton planted, it was cottonchopping time. Every man, woman, and kid big enough to carry a hoe went to the field until all the cotton was finished. This kept us busy until about the 4th of July. Then it was laying by time. There was not much to do until time to start fodderpulling in August.

On the 4th of July the whole community would have a fish fry. The men and boys would go seining first. Then, the ladies would come in a wagon later with the children. They'd bring the washpots and frying pans to cook the hush puppies and fish in. We'd carry in the first fish we caught. Somebody would dress them and have them ready when the ladies got there. Then while the ladies cooked, we'd seine some more, right up till about suppertime. After we ate, we'd divide equally the fish that hadn't been fried so everybody had some to carry on home.

Unfortunately, school picked up again for the month of July. Even though I hated school, I worked hard and made the basketball and the football teams. I would play rough if I had to. I stayed on the basketball team until I almost killed a boy. Then I quit and played only football. Later, I started with the baseball team and stayed with that team until I quit school at the end of the ninth grade. I was the catcher for the team. Our gloves and mits weren't the best, and I played a lot with a broken finger; but I'd stay in the game as long as I could. After I quit school, I started a team with the boys in the community. I was still the catcher and Pete Carson was the pitcher. We would play on Saturday afternoons and were known as the Country Boys.

Other things had to be taken care of on Saturday, too, like going to the mill. And you weren't allowed to swap your corn for meal. You had to stay there while your corn was being ground. Sometimes having to wait was a hardship. It would make you late for the ball game. So, I would swap our corn for meal already ground and ask the miller not to tell Papa. But this did not work for long. I learned that waiting was better than trying to play ball with a sore backside, as Papa believed that honesty came first.

Fall.

Fodderpulling began around the first of August and lasted for three or four weeks. Several of the farmers would swap. As one man's corn was ready, we would pull his fodder. Then another field would be ready, and we'd all go there. It was like this until everybody's fodder was in the barn.

Mama did a lot of canning in the summer and fall. We grew everything we ate. It was nothing to find a hundred or more jars of green beans in the pantry, maybe a hundred or more jars of tomatoes and vegetable soup. There might also be seventy-five pounds of dried apples and peaches from our trees in the orchard. Nothing was allowed to go to waste. We had a room out on the front porch where we put the apples to dry for the winter. Any apples that couldn't be used to dry or can were picked up and fed to the hogs.

Mama always had a hill of sweet potatoes out on the edge of the backyard. They were handy for her to get to. She'd leave the cotton field late in the afternoon while we were weighing up. She'd go to the house, stopping by the potato hill to dig some big old sweet potatoes. She'd carry them home, peel them, and put them in a pot to stew. We'd come in from the field, and there would be stewed sweet potatoes and a big bowl of cream gravy for supper.

We'd pick cotton in the fall; and then when cold weather came, it was time to kill a cow and a hog. This was the most enjoyable time of the year. We had fresh meat! The family could eat half a cow in a week, or maybe even less than a week. We had something to eat at all times, but it was not always exactly what we wanted. But during beef- and hog-killing time we lived like kings.

When we killed hogs, we'd make sausage, cook it, and put it in jars to save for the summer. These jars were stacked in the pantry off the kitchen. It was hard to keep a boy out of these goodies, and especially when I would spend the day pulling a boat up and down Flint River or following my hounds over the hills and through the bottoms. I guess what I brought home from the river and the woods helped repay for all the jars of sausage that I stole. I hope so.

Around November we made syrup from our sugar cane. A man has never really lived until he has his plate full of ribbon-cane syrup, puts a big slab of real butter on that plate, mixes up the syrup and butter and then pulls a biscuit through it. By the time you've pulled six or seven biscuits through your plate, you can say you've had a good breakfast!

We also made our sugar from the ribbon-cane syrup. At the bottom of the barrel, the syrup would turn to sugar. This was taken out and put in a clean white sock, hung up and let drip for several days. Then water was poured in the sock, and it dripped for another three or four days. (This water was saved and vinegar was made from it.) The sugar would by this time be pure white. This then was ground through an old-fashioned sausage mill; out would come some of the best cane sugar a person could ever want.

We made our own hominy, too. We'd take the corn off the cob and put it in a washpot. Then we'd put lye that came out of the ashes that we saved during the winter onto the corn. (We'd save the ashes in an ash hopper. It was built wide at the top and narrow at the bottom and was made out of a log.) You'd pour the lye over the corn, and it would take the husk off and just leave the inside. Then you'd wash the corn until there was no trace of lye whatsoever. After this, the corn was white and clear; and then you'd have good hominy.

On one of the first rainy days in the fall Nonie and I would make our chewing tobacco. (Nonie and I had started chewing tobacco when each of us was six.) We grew our own tobacco. We'd strip that tobacco and stem it. Then we'd take sweet Scotch snuff and put a layer of tobacco and a layer of snuff and another layer of tobacco and twist it together. We had a big rock out near the chimney. I'd raise the rock and Nonie would put the tobacco under it. We'd leave it there until it was packed firm and tight. A lot of times we'd put a couple of twists in the vice at the blacksmith's shop between two boards. Every day we'd go down and tighten the vice. That was our Sunday tobacco that we used when we had company. It looked really good because it was flat and hard. You weren't ashamed to offer somebody else a chew of that! We made certain to make up enough tobacco in the winter to last us through the next summer because every man in the family chewed, and he chewed everyday.

On Thanksgiving everybody in the community would gather to make what was called a rabbit stew. It was a sight. Sometimes we'd have twenty or thirty rabbits to put in a big black washpot out in the yard. We'd build a fire under this pot. There would be fresh pork in the stew, too, and chickens, with corn and tomatoes. We would make maybe twenty or thirty gallons. The ladies would also cook pumpkin and mincemeat pies and cakes of every kind. There would be a big crowd—four or five families together—and we enjoyed it every year.

W inter.

Christmas was always a time of visiting and serenading. Papa always made sure he had plenty of peach brandy and corn whiskey for the holidays. (He made this year-round in the stills out by the edge of the woods.) The boys and men would dress up in old clothes, paint their faces, or wear a mask made from a flour sack. They would go from house to house, shooting fire crackers and guns.

Every home was open to them. Cake, coffee, and spirits were served. After they serenaded a house and ate and drank, the men would go on to the next house, which was maybe a couple of miles on down the road. Some of the group would get past going—the liquor would get to them—and they would be left at someone's house. A wagon would come along and pick them up and go on to find someone else that needed help. This would end around midnight.

On Christmas morning, the menfolk would either come to our house or go to the Carsons or Hardys or Padgetts and have eggnog. The way they would make it was to take a number two washtub and break a couple dozen eggs in it. Then they'd put in a lot of sugar and pour in about five gallons of homemade whiskey. They'd stir this mixture up. At our house, they'd sit around the fireplace in the kitchen, drinking egg-nog, chewing tobacco, and telling tales.

Papa wouldn't let us kids taste the eggnog. But I'd watch him and when he got to talking thick-lipped, I'd slip around and crawl under the table. When nobody was dipping from the wash-tub, which was sitting on the floor underneath the table, I'd take the dipper and drink my fill. So I enjoyed eggnog right along with the rest of them.

A big dinner was served on Christmas, and then things went back to normal on the day after. The men went back to work, gathering corn, cutting wood. It was time for the year to start round again.

***In 1925, the year that Tommie was** seventeen, Georgia had its worse drought since 1845, making the outlook for the future of farming even more dismal than it had been. Georgia citizens, young and old alike, began to look elsewhere for a way to make their living. Many went North to work in industries that were booming. Tommie did the same.*

THE MICHIGAN MONEY TREE

The first crop I ever had was a cotton crop. Papa gave me and Nonie two acres each to farm for our own when I was seventeen. I planted mine in cotton and made two and a half bales. I sold the cotton for thirty-five or thirty-six cents a pound and got around $130. That was the most money I had ever had! I bought my winter clothes and a pair of shoes out of the money and saved the rest. I had plans for next spring. I would take the money I had left and go to Michigan to find the Michigan money tree. We had two cousins up there, and they were the biggest liars in seven states. They would come back to the farm and tell you about the heaven that Michigan was, that money was hanging on trees.

So I decided to go up there and get rich. I told Mama that I wanted to go. She said, "You'd better ask your Papa. If you leave without telling him, you'll never get to come home again." I dreaded asking Papa because I knew he would want me to stay and work on the farm. But the night before I planned to go, I said, "Papa, what would you think about me going up to Michigan and earning some money for the summer?" Papa surprised me. He didn't say I couldn't go. Instead, he said, "Well, if you think you can do better. . . ." The next morning Papa took me in the old truck down to the Broad Street Depot in Griffin. I bought a one-way ticket from Griffin to Muskegon, Michigan.

There was a song everybody was singing then called "I Am Going to Buy Me a Ticket As Long As I Am Tall." And that's what I did. When the man behind the wicket window handed me my ticket and I unfolded it, one end was on the floor while the portion I was reading was in my hand.

I had never spent a night away from home, so the trip was an ordeal. I made it fine until I got to Chicago. It was getting dark, and I got so homesick that the whole rest of the trip I sat in my train seat and cried. A lady sitting nearby tried to console me; but that made it even worse, since I was so bashful and shy.

The trip took all day and most of the night. Finally, I arrived in Michigan in the wee hours of the morning. I stayed at the depot the rest of the night. About daylight my cousin came and got me.

I discovered right away that they had pulled up all of the money trees in Michigan. So, I went to work at the Lakey Foundry making cores for automobile motors—straight eight Studebakers, Durants, and Buicks. We made these cores out of sand. We put the sand in a molding block and poured ore over it. The molding block was shaped like a motor. A tractor would come along and carry the molds down to the furnace where about 120 would be put on a rack and burned. You got paid by the piece. Once in a while a big motor in the assembly plant would come on about the time your molds got put on the rack in the furnace. The motor would shake the whole floor. You could lose the whole rack that way and get nothing for your work.

I wasn't so homesick after I went to work. I worked in Michigan for the spring and summer and went back home to hunt and fish in the winter. I returned to Michigan each spring for two more seasons, working at the Brunswick Baltic Radio Company the second spring and at Continental Motor Company the third.

I had never seen a radio much less turned one on; but when the foreman at Brunswick Baltic Radio Company asked me if I knew how to inspect one, I assured him I did. As soon as he left, I asked the guy working next to me, "What am I supposed to do?" He said, "Give an okay to so many and knock so many out." There was a little key that we used to turn the knobs. I didn't know how the radio was supposed to sound, so I did what my co-worker said. Every so many radios I'd send through, and every so many I'd reject. I don't know what happened to those radios when they got out into people's homes.

At Continental Motors I milled flange off the motors, getting the rough pieces off the sides. That was an exacting job because if you set your milling machine too deep you'd ruin the block. Set it right, and the block would be good.

The first year I lived with our cousins for a few weeks and then boarded with another couple. The second and third working seasons I lived with some relatives.

At seventeen, I guess I looked good to the girls, but I would not date any of the girls who were in the neighborhood. The first summer I was there my landlady made a date for me with the girl next door. I finally got up enough courage to go over, and during the evening the girl offered me a glass of root beer, which I had never tasted. It was so bad that I knew she was trying to poison me, so I never went back.

The second and third springs I was in Michigan I lived next door to a family who owned a large furniture store. They invited me over to eat hot baked bread. In the family was a beautiful daughter. She was a good help in her father's store. Her dad liked me and took a lot of time with me, even offering me a job. But I refused the job because the girl was always around.

A country boy gone to town—such a life was not made for me. I would rather follow a pack of hounds through the river swamp. So, when Mama wrote that they needed me, I made plans to go home. When I went over to tell the family next door that I was leaving for Georgia, the father offered to give me half interest in his store if I would stay on and marry his daughter. That was too much. I left for home a week early.

✝

The house where Tommie was born.
Granddad's family.

Front l-r: Sallie Harper, Asa Harper's wife; Asa Harper, Tommie's uncle;
A. G. Harper, Tommie's cousin (child standing); Lela Harper, Tommie's
uncle; Susan Harper, Tommie's grandmother; John Harper, Tommie's
granddad.
Back l-r: Frank Harper, Tommie's papa; Dave Gable, cousin raised by
Frank and Willie; Will Harper, Tommie's uncle.

Frank Harper, Tommie's papa.   Willie Harper, Tommie's mama.

Tommie's family.

Front l-r: Tommie, Blanche, Nannie
Back l-r: Nonie, Papa, Mama.

Tommie as a baby.

Papa and Mama dressed up.

Papa and Mama in the field.

The community gathers for rabbit stew at Thanksgiving.

Tommie in Michigan.

PART
II

TRAINING
1932–1947

Now know I that the Lord saveth his anointed; he will hear him from his holy heaven with the saving strength of his right hand.

Psalms 20:6

Tommie returned to Brooks from

Michigan in 1929, when he was twenty-one. He began farming immediately, working to get the family's farm out of debt and to make some money for them and for himself. At night and on the weekends he hunted and fished. On the weekends, too, he often boxed. Promoters would come through the community bringing boxing gloves and a promise of seventy-five cents to the winner and fifty cents to the loser. A crowd would gather. Finally, two country boys wearing overalls and no shirts would step into the ring. Tommie was usually one of them.

*   *   *

Tommie Harper had been "up North." That made him cut a special figure in the eyes of the Fayette County community. He was what you might call a "local celebrity," even if on most occasions he had more notoriety than fame.

He rode a big black horse and packed a pistol. Tommie was the community hellion. When there was any trouble that needed to be handled, it was Tommie Harper people called. His path was one nobody wanted to cross. This all changed when he fell in love.

HOW I MET THE GIRL WHO
BECAME MY WIFE

Mama had written me in Michigan,
"Come home, son. We need you on the farm."

So I had gone home.

I went to farming again. I farmed Papa's
place and then rented a farm from a fellow Hand
and farmed the two farms together. I gave Papa
everything made on his place and kept for myself what I made on the Hand place. When I
came home, Papa was deep in debt and about to

lose the farm. Now, three years later, I had paid off the debt; the farm was free and clear.

It was about Christmas time. They were practicing a play over at County Line Christian Church. (Services were held at the County Line church once a month; Sunday School was taught every Sunday—sometimes in the morning and sometimes in the afternoon.) The young people of the community looked at the church as a place to go to visit and just get together, as there wasn't much to do for entertainment otherwise. I never went, but Nonie did.

Nonie had a part in this play they were doing for Christmas. He asked me one night if I wanted to go watch them practice. So I went.

There on the church rostrum I saw Rachel for the first time. She had a part in the play. I thought she was about the prettiest girl I had ever seen.

When the practice was over, Rachel said to me, "Why don't you come to Sunday School next Sunday?" I mumbled something about I might if I could get my clothes out of the cleaners. I had no intention of going to Sunday School; but as the week passed, I thought more and more about it. For some reason, the next Sunday I went to church.

A friendship with Rachel began. We took a liking to each other and began sitting together at Sunday School. It kept building up and building up, and finally about spring I got up enough courage to ask Rachel Leach for a date. I asked her if I could walk her home after Sunday School. This was the first time I had ever asked a girl for a date.

When I asked Rachel if I could walk her home, she said, "I'll have to ask my mother." It was a nervous few minutes before Rachel returned, but then all was okay. Margie Leach had said yes. So Rachel and I walked the quarter-mile from the church to her house.

As I was walking on home after leaving Rachel off, I began to talk to myself.

"Now, if you're going to try to go with this sweet young girl (Rachel was fourteen, and I was twenty-four), then hadn't you better straighten up and act a little different? How would you want a boy to be who was dating one of your sisters?"

I knew the answer to that. So I decided before I ever got home that day, "I'm going to be to this girl what I would expect a boy to be to one of my sisters. I'm going to reform."

And I did reform then and there. I quit drinking. Quit cursing. Quit carousing around and staying out all night. But it would be a long time—in fact, several years—before I'd do any more than reform.

*   *   *

Rachel and I would date by walking home from Sunday School. Then after we got to know each other a little better, I'd go in the house for a visit. As things progressed I would stay over at the Leach house on Sundays until bedtime— which was always nine o'clock sharp. (Rachel's mother had to call bedtime on me only once in the three years Rachel and I went together.)

The Leaches had a nice front porch with a swing; Rachel and I enjoyed that. They also had a "front room," a parlor with a fireplace. This room was across the hall from the rest of the house. In it there was a Victrola which you cranked by hand. It played big records. We'd listen to such songs as "My Blue Heaven," "Red River Valley," "When the Moon Comes Over the Mountain," and "I'll Be Loving You Always." While these songs were playing, we'd be holding hands. Rachel would usually serve some refreshments, like cake and iced tea (if they had any ice), and, if not, cold well water. Almost all of our courting was done this way—by sitting together at church and at Rachel's house.

One time I asked Rachel if she would like to go to the circus in Griffin. I borrowed Papa's Model T truck, and we went. We enjoyed it a lot.

The only trouble we had occurred when Rachel thought she ought to be seeing some other boys. She'd have a date with J. D. Hudgins, and that would make me so mad. I'd go into Griffin to see my sister Nannie, who was by now married to Jack Hambrick. We'd get in their Model A with the rumble seat and go by and pick up Rachel Harrison as my date.

"Where do you want to drive?" Jack would ask.

"Let's go out to Brooks," I'd say.

Of course, we'd have to drive right by Rachel's house, and she'd see Rachel Harrison and me in the rumble seat. That would get her real interested in me again. (One time I bought her a dresser set—a brush, comb, and mirror— and I found out later that J. D. Hudgins had bought her one just like it!)

Once we had a fuss on Sunday night and parted mad. I worried all night long. The next morning before I went to the field I hurried over to Bill Huckaby's store. I bought a box of candy and took it to Rachel bright and early, before the school bus arrived. I apologized, and she apologized; all was well again.

CHICAGO OR MARRIED LIFE

Rachel and I dated for about three years. During that time I got very interested in bettering myself in life. There were not many books, magazines, or newspapers in our home. A tri-weekly newspaper was about what we had. But when my Granddad would visit his brother in Union City, Georgia, he would bring home magazines that his brother had given him. His brother was a railroad man, and he would find these papers left on the train.

In one such paper there was a notice: Forest Rangers Needed. I answered the advertisement and was soon on my way to becoming a forest ranger. This was when the government had first begun to establish national parks. They put out these correspondence courses which you could complete to prepare for taking the civil service examination to become a forest ranger. If you finished the course and passed the final interview and examination, the government promised you a job.

For a dollar you could get enough lessons to last you for a month. I'd send them a dollar money order the first of every month to order my lessons. You sent in each lesson as you completed it. When you sent in your lesson, you either passed or you didn't. If you did well, they'd send you some extra material free. I always looked forward to that.

There were lessons on the purpose of national parks, on timber, population, fire prevention, and tourism. There were arithmetic problems such as, "How many board feet are there in a twenty-five acre stand of timber?" (The forest ranger was also responsible for overseeing the cutting of timber.) I studied at night and on the weekend, sitting with my charts and maps at the kitchen table.

When I finished the correspondence course, it was time to go to the Post Office in Griffin to be interviewed. After the interview, there were three tests. About nine other people were being interviewed and taking the final tests the day I was. You had so many minutes to do each test.

Then you turned in your paper, and the man in charge graded the tests while you waited. Since you were guaranteed a job if you passed the interview and tests, you waited with bated breath.

The man graded my three tests and came out to where I was waiting in the hall.

He said, "Mr. Harper, you passed. You'll be hearing from the government about a position as a forest ranger within the next few weeks."

I was happy.

I began to watch the mail every day. Finally, the letter arrived. The government had sent my job placement. I would be a forest ranger in the new Yellowstone National Park. Everybody in the family, me included, thought that was too far for a farm boy to be going. So I wrote back and asked could they give me a second choice closer to home. The government wrote back and offered a forest ranger's position at Chickamauga National Park, which was a hundred and forty miles away from Brooks. I thought I'd take that one, but Mama said, "Tom, if you go that far away to work permanently, you'll never get back home." So the farmer went right on farming, fishing, and hunting. I didn't take the job.

A few months later, though, I saw another advertisement. This one said: "Radio and Electronics. Good men needed to learn the use of this up-and-coming business." Talking movies were big now and radios were becoming more and more widespread; so this looked like something that could build up to be a great future in a young man's life.

I took the course. There were lots of figures, numbers, and diagrams. You had to study charts and then draw how to hook this thing up with that to make connections. I studied hard, did one lesson a week, and mailed it in to the government. When I finished the course, I went this time to the Spalding County Courthouse in Griffin to take my tests and have my interview. It was with the Department of Public Transportation. I passed the interview and the tests. "We have a place for you in Chicago," the government said. This time I was going. I knew by now that I did not want to do what I was doing for the rest of my life.

*   *   *

Rachel and I were in our third year of dating. She would soon graduate from high school. (Rachel was both valedictorian and class poet of the senior class!) So I asked her to marry me. Her first statement was, "I can't get married. I've got to finish school." I said, "I meant let's get married when you get out of school." She still hesitated. Finally, she said yes. I went down to Winn's Jewelry Store in Griffin and bought her a diamond ring. I gave the ring to her the day she graduated, but I still couldn't get her to set a date.

One Sunday in August, soon after I had gotten the job assignment in Chicago, Rachel and I were walking to church. I made her an offer: "I will go to Chicago and take the job, and then I'll come back down here and get you." She thought so little of that offer that she turned it down. The next Sunday I made her another offer: "We will get married before Christmas, or I will go to work in Chicago." I requested that she give me her answer in a week, and she agreed to do so. The next Sunday, walking to church, Rachel said, "Would October 13 be okay with you?"

There were two things I had left to do. I had to let Rachel know what we were in for as a young married couple, and I had to ask her daddy if we could get married. The Sunday she set the date we went in the afternoon to a singing at a church in a neighboring community. During the singing, we went outside and sat in a car to talk.

I said to Rachel, "I want you to know how much money I have. All I've got is $64. That won't be much when we get married."

Rachel said, "That's all right. We'll make do on that. We'll get by."

When we got back to Rachel's house, I screwed up my courage to ask her daddy if we could get married. Her mother and daddy were sitting around on the side porch, so I walked up on the front porch, through the house, and out onto the side porch. I was too nervous to sit down.

I leaned up against a post and said, "Rachel and I have . . . I want to ask you a question, and I want an answer. Rachel and I have decided that we'll get married. Is it all right?"

Rachel's mother quickly spoke up, "You'll have to be good to her, Tom Harper."

And her daddy answered back, "Well, Margie, you know he'll do that."

The conversation got a little better after that, and they agreed. Rachel and I were set to get married.

Rachel and her mother got busy get-
ting ready for the wedding. They traded eggs for dress
material, which was ten and fifteen cents a yard at Mr.
Buck Lee's store in Digby. (Digby, the community where
Rachel lived, was a couple of miles from Brooks and had
a population of twenty-eight people.) In September when
school began, Rachel and her mother caught the school
bus one day and went into Griffin to buy Rachel's wedding dress. They chose a brown dress with a Peter Pan
double collar, one white and one pale orange. Rachel also
got some brown, lace-up dress shoes, a brown hat with a
turned-up brim in front, and a blue winter coat. Margie,
Rachel's mother, was working that fall at the Griffin Po-
mona Products Company; this made it possible for her to
buy Rachel these store-bought things. When Rachel and
Margie finished shopping, they met Mr. Carl Crowder,
the school bus driver, and went back home on the school
bus. On their wedding day Rachel would be just two
weeks short of seventeen years of age; Tommie was
twenty-seven.

RACHEL AND I GET MARRIED

There was excitement around the Harper homeplace on October 13, 1935. Everybody
was up early on this Sunday morning. The cows
had to be milked and the mules, hogs, and chick-

ens had to be watered and fed. When the work was finished outside, we went in for a good breakfast of hot biscuits, butter, syrup, and strong coffee—which some of the family needed. (Tommie, for sure!)

We had taken our baths on Saturday night. But this morning the men had to shave. Then the real rush was on. The whole family had to get their clothes and find a place to get dressed. Everything had to be just right, for the wedding was to take place at four o'clock at Nannie and Jack's house in Griffin.

When we all got dressed, the old Model T truck was made ready: oil checked, water put in the radiator, chairs put in the back. The Harpers were ready to go by and pick up the bride and her family.

Then the trip started into Griffin with the bridegroom driving, the bride sitting beside him, his papa on the outside in the cab. Everybody else, including Rachel's friend Edna who had come down on the train from Atlanta, was in the chairs in the back of the truck.

Arriving in Griffin, the menfolk sat outside telling their stories of bygone days; the womenfolk helped fix dinner. This was a nervous time for the young couple. The bride stayed with the womenfolk; the groom with the men—until he got so nervous he and his brother walked up to town and back. You will remember that this was the young man that could face the darkest night, fight his way out of trouble, stand his ground with any of the roughnecks of the community. But look at him now—nervous, afraid of the hours to come when he would take as his wife the girl he had courted for three years.

At two o'clock I drove two miles to Sunnyside to get Reverend A. J. Mize, the minister who was to marry us. I had paid Reverend Mize the afternoon before. When I had asked him earlier how much he would charge for a wedding, he had said, "I'd like to be paid with a possum. That's good eating, a possum."

So I caught a possum down at the foot of Harper Mountain. The dogs treed him, and I shook the tree. The possum fell out and "sulled." A good dog will leave a "sulling" possum alone, and then the hunter can just reach down and catch him. I penned the possum up for a couple of weeks to fatten him up. Then on Saturday before the wedding, I took the possum up to the preacher's house to pay him in advance for marrying Rachel and me.

At four o'clock the minister said, "It's time for the wedding." This big brave man stood with his little ninety-eight pound girl sweetheart before the fireplace, which Nannie had decorated with ferns—his knees shaking, his voice trembling. I said "I will" to all the questions the minister asked me.

I remember especially one question: "Do you take this woman till death do you part?" I promised, "I will," which are the strongest words in the English language. (Mama sat on the bed in an adjoining room. She was thrilled over the wedding but just did not participate in any of her children's weddings.) The minister said a few more words, and we became Mr. and Mrs. Tommie Frank Harper.

We attended church that night with Nannie and Jack. This time, however, we went not as a young couple in love but as a young married couple. Our honeymoon on Monday morning was a train ride from Griffin back out to Brooks. We attended the funeral of Rachel's aunt on Monday afternoon. From the funeral we went to our new home, which consisted of two rooms in Rachel's family's house.

We had furnished these rooms with a new unfinished clothes closet, a chest of drawers and a bed that the bride's mother gave us, a small flat-top cookstove and a kitchen cabinet given us by the groom's mother, and a fifty-pound icebox which was also given to us. (The ice truck ran by our house twice a week. We would buy fifty pounds of ice each time to keep the food from spoiling.) Our entire supply of money was $64, but we were happy and never went hungry.

On Tuesday morning we walked two miles to Papa's where we spent the day. I broke and hauled corn. We then walked back the two miles that night. That was the routine each day until the crop was gathered. On Saturdays we went to Griffin with a load of wood for Papa. This would give us a chance to get five pounds of sausage for breakfast the next week, and sometimes we would be able to get a mess of mullet fish for Saturday night supper.

Then came winter and woodcutting. I helped Papa with the wood and in return he suggested that I take a load home as was needed for Rachel's family and also for our own use.

The next spring Rachel and I started farming for ourselves. Before long we had our own cow, hogs, and chickens. We had a good milk cow; this gave us fresh butter and milk. The young chickens were big enough for frying. This gave us meat to enjoy as we worked the farm. On a rainy day we would take a fryer and go up to Granny Leach's house (she was Rachel's grandmother) and enjoy dinner with her. This was the beginning of our years together.

In her seventeenth, eighteenth, and
nineteenth years Rachel learned to be a farmer's wife.
She took care of the house. She cooked dinner each day,
taking it to Tommie in the field if he did not have time to
come to the house. She canned the sausages she and
Tommie bought in Griffin every Saturday, one pint for
each day of the week. She sewed their clothes, even Tom-
mie's shorts. They had a running battle over those shorts:
because she knew only the fundamentals of sewing,
Rachel did not make a buttonhole and sew on a button
to fasten the shorts. Instead, the shorts fastened with a
shingle nail. This was not to Tommie's liking. "It's embar-
rassing to have to fasten your shorts with a shingle nail,"
Tommie would complain. But until Rachel got instruc-
tions in how to make buttonholes, Tommie had to use
the little sharp nail.

Rachel also took on chores outside the house. She
fed the chickens, and she tried to learn to milk the cow.

RACHEL ON THE FARM

Rachel told me one day not long after we got married, "I want to learn to milk the cow. That way I could already have the milk and be churning before you get home from the field." So the next day we went to the barn for her to have her lesson in how to milk.

I put a stool beside the cow, Rachel sat down on it, and I showed her what to do. She caught on fast. Everything seemed to be in order, so I went to get corn for the mules. In just a minute or two, though, I heard a commotion. It was Rachel. She had jumped up so fast that she had kicked the milk stool over. Now she was standing in the middle of the barn, just sobbing. I hurried to where she was. "What in the world is wrong, Rachel?" I asked. "What happened?"

Finally, she stopped crying enough to let me know what terrible thing had happened while she was milking. "The cow looked at me," Rachel said. "She turned her head around and kept looking at me." That was Rachel's first and last time to try milking. I could tell that chore was not for her.

* * *

Rachel worked hard to make our house look nice. Our source of heat was the fireplace. We had a big flat smooth stone laid on cement that served as the hearth. How to keep this hearth clean with all the tobacco chewing and snuff dipping that went on? This was a daily problem.

Now everyone knows about the red mud of Georgia, but there was also white mud. White mud was not as plentiful, but every once in a while you could find a bank with streaks of white mud.

Rachel searched until she found a bank like this on the roadside down below our house. After I went to the field, she'd take an empty gallon syrup bucket and a hoe or a rake and go "digging for white mud." She would dig only the white part, which was a tedious job, since red clay would be present, too. When she'd get about half a bucket full, she'd bring it home, put water in the bucket, and make a thin, white paste. This then was used on the hearth and side fronts of the fireplace.

Rachel would take a rag which stayed in the bucket of mud and smear or paint the hearthstone. When it dried, it would be snow-white! She'd almost dare anyone to mess it up. Of course, this smearing and painting had to be done daily. So, Rachel would set the white mud bucket, water, and rag somewhere easy to get to, and we would use that batch of mud until it "lost its whiteness." It would stay in good shape for a fairly long time. We'd add water each time and mix it up good. When it finally got down to "blue john" and had lost its whiteness, Rachel and some other women and girls in the community would go digging again. It would always be a fun time with family or friends all walking down the country road.

In the wintertime it wouldn't take the hearth but a few minutes to dry because of the heat from the roaring fire in the fireplace. In the summertime the hearth stayed cleaner longer because the fireplace wasn't used except when Rachel heated the flatirons on ironing day.

I WAS A TROUBLED MAN

It was 1938. Rachel and I had now been married almost three years. Our farm was prospering, and we were happy. But something was bothering me. I was a troubled man.

Although I had reformed more than six years earlier when I met Rachel, I went to church only as a formality. I would see men at the County Line Christian Church sit out on the steps and make jokes about God and then get up to go inside to serve communion. I had decided that religious talk was just that—talk and not much more.

Whatever was disturbing me got worse when somebody in the community died. I was always willing to go help dig the grave. But as I put the shovel into the earth and threw the loads of dirt over my shoulder, I could not rid myself of those questions from childhood. I would think of those nights sitting around the fire when Papa would be out on a drinking spree or taking the law into his own hands with other men. I'd remember Mama reading from the Bible and praying that Papa would get home safe and that there would be no trouble in the community. She would always read about people being dead. And even now, at thirty years of age, I would still ask myself when we menfolk would be digging a grave, "How can people stay dead so long? And who will rise at the judgment day and who won't?" I was haunted by these questions. I wondered what they meant for a rough man like me.

I'd come in from the fields and while Rachel was preparing supper, I would sit in front of the fire and read. I'd alternate between two books—my latest western and the Bible. I'd read one chapter in the western, which I'd buy for a penny when Rachel and I delivered wood in Griffin on Saturday or which I'd get by swapping books with the Hudgins boys; and I'd read one chapter in the Bible, which Blanche and Nannie had given me for my birthday one year. I was searching for peace.

What Tommie Harper did not know

was that a religious revival had been stirring for many decades throughout the United States and would soon reach even to Brooks and Digby, Georgia. This revival had its roots in a much earlier time.

In the years following the Civil War, the Methodist Church sounded a call for a return to godliness, to the principles of their founder, John Wesley: the use of the "mourner's bench" for penitent sinners, study meetings for the "perfection of the saints," and camp meetings for the benefit of sinners and saints alike. In 1867 a crusade for holiness in the Methodist Church began.

Holiness meant living a life free of sin, pure, undefiled, strict, separate from the world. Individuals could live this kind of clean, devout, and holy life if they had received sanctification, a "second grace" experienced as a definite work of grace. The Methodist crusade for holiness was a crusade for emphasis on sanctification.

In 1867, an invitation was issued for all those interested in "holding a camp meeting, the special object of which should be the promotion of the work of entire sanctification." This invitation resulted in the formation of "The National Camp Meeting Association for the Promotion of Christian Holiness." The well-known Methodist pastor, the Reverend Alfred Cookman, addressed an invitation to all who, irrespective of denominational ties, "feel themselves comparatively isolated in their profession of holiness" to come together to hold a meeting to "promote holiness, furnish an illustration of evangelical union, and make common application of the descent of the Spirit upon ourselves, the church, the nation, and the world." When this camp meeting opened in Vineland, New Jersey, on July 17, 1867, the modern holiness movement in the United States was begun.

This camp meeting was a success. Many participants received the second blessing of sanctification. A call was made for another camp meeting to be held the following year. Between 1867 and 1883 a total of fifty-two of these camp meetings was held, mostly on Methodist campgrounds. (During the height of the holiness movement, 200 of the 240 ministers of the Methodist North Georgia Conference testified to having received the experience of sanctification as a "second blessing.")

In the late 1880s, however, opposition to the holiness movement arose in the Methodist Church. As the controversy continued, many of those who practiced holiness began to leave the Methodist Church to organize their own congregations. (Other congregations, such as the Baptists, also experienced an exodus of individuals committed to practicing the holiness life.)

It was some of these congregations which would later become Pentecostal churches. Although they started out as small and struggling congregations meeting in homes, schoolhouses, and out of doors, their influence and presence would subsequently spread throughout the world. Authorities estimate that in the United States today the number of persons who would be classified as Pentecostals totals at least four million. The estimate of the number of Pentecostals world-wide ranges from a conservative eight to twelve million to The World Council of Churches' estimate of thirty-five million. Pentecostalism has been called the Third Force in Christianity (the Protestant and Roman Catholic movements being the other two) and continues to be the fastest growing religious body in the world. The Presbyterian writer Charles Sydnor, Jr. has stated that the Pentecostal movement "is an authentic, reformation-revival of historic significance, equal with those other great movements of centuries past."

It was a Pentecostal group, the Congregational Holiness Church, who came in 1938 to the Brooks and Digby community to set up a tent and hold a revival.

This group, like other Pentecostal denominations which had been flourishing since the early 1900s, believed in the infallibility of the Bible, in the Trinity, the virgin birth and complete deity of Christ, the atoning sacrifice of His death for the sins of the world, the Resurrection, and the return of Christ in bodily form to earth. They taught that individuals could be sanctified and attain holiness in their daily lives. Like other Pentecostal churches, the Congregational Holiness group which came to Brooks preached that all believers may receive the baptism of the Holy Spirit, accompanied by speaking in tongues. (Speaking in tongues meant speaking in a language entirely unknown and foreign to the speaker.) The Pentecostals believed receiving the baptism of the Holy Spirit prepared one for living a new life, a life marked by such traits as wisdom, kindness, discernment, healing, and love.

This Pentecostal doctrine and these holiness practices were new to the Brooks and Digby community. There was much speculation, curiosity, and skepticism when the Congregational Holiness group put up their tent.

THE NIGHT I GOT CONVERTED

In June of 1938 a group known as Congregational Holiness came out from Griffin to our community. The group put up a tent and started a revival, not far from our house. The whole community was against the revival. Mama was talking to Rachel's mother, standing out in front of the County Line Christian Church one Sunday right after the tent was put up. Mama said, "I sure hope that bunch don't cause division in the community." And Rachel's mother replied, "Oh, all they'll get is the scum." Rachel and I, as it turned out, were some of the community that tent revival got!

Like many others, I didn't want this revival in our community. So my plans were to slip over to the tent during the night and cut the ropes. But news of strange happenings drew many of us in the community to come and see what was going on. I decided I'd go satisfy my curiosity, and then I'd cut the ropes. I was determined that I'd run these people off.

When Rachel and I went over to see what was going on, we didn't understand what we saw. These people were strange in their worship service. Everyone would pray loud at the same time, making the strangest sounds which they called "speaking in tongues." They would shout up and down the aisles, laying hands on the people that were sick. These sick people would then cry, "God has touched me. I am healed." The people would sing, and it was some of the best singing anybody had ever heard. There'd be more shouting and speaking in tongues while the preacher started to preach. This would make cold chills run up and down your spine. It would make you think, "If I don't go to the altar, the devil will get me before I get home." Rachel and I went to the meeting every night. I forgot that I had planned to cut the ropes on the tent.

*   *   *

The revival was in its third week. Rachel and I had now been going every night. One evening when we were walking down the road to the tent, Rachel said, "Why don't we help out? Why don't we invite the preacher and her husband home for dinner tomorrow?" I agreed, so we asked Brother and Sister Akins to come for dinner the next day.

The date was July 11, 1938. When the Akins came over, they asked no questions about our religious beliefs. They didn't talk to us about getting saved. They only talked about how good the Lord was and what great things He had done in their lives. Brother Akins told us how mean he had been and how miraculous it was that God had saved him.

When dinner was over and the visit ended, Rachel and I were left to think on what we had heard. We did not know anything about conviction, but the impression the evangelist and her husband had left was deep in our hearts. When I went to tend the stock that afternoon, walking down the path to the barn, I thought, "I would not go to the altar tonight for $1,000. The boys in the community would be sure to say, 'That preacher got ahold of him today.'"

When the feeding and milking were over, Rachel and I ate supper and got ready for the meeting. As we walked up to the tent, our neighbor, Mr. Walt Hudgins, was walking round and round in a circle in front of the tent.

He came up to me and said, "Tom, it would be nobody's business but mine if I went to that altar tonight, would it?" And then he turned and, with his hands behind his back, started walking again. I started walking in a circle right behind him.

Rachel and I had moved up one seat each week the revival had been in progress. We were now sitting on the third bench from the back. While I stopped to talk to Mr. Hudgins, Rachel went on in under the tent and took a seat. But this time she went way down near the front. Some of the boys said, "She's got you now. You'll have to go down front." I replied, "No, I won't. She'll sit by herself tonight."

When the service started, I went around to
the side of the tent and sat on a 2x6 board laid
across two stove wood blocks. I don't remember
much of anything that happened in that service.
I can only tell you the first song they sang: "He's
the Lily of the Valley, the Bright and Morning Star.
He's the Fairest of Ten Thousand to my Soul."

The closer it got to the end of the service,
the more I knew I was going to that altar. I was
just waiting for the preacher to give the altar call.
But, even then, I planned to be as inconspicuous
as possible. I thought, "I'll kneel right here at the
end of the altar nearest me." When the altar call
was given, however, I got up and, instead of stopping at the closest end, I went all the way across
the front of the tent and knelt at the far end of
the altar.

Something happened that I never under-
stood. I didn't know what to say when I got to the
altar. I didn't know how to pray. All I could think
to say was, "God, if you can save a man like
Brother Akins, I know you can save me." I don't
know what I said after that. I don't know what I
thought. I only know that when I got up, I was
a changed man. Everything around me had
changed. The people looked different. The sur-
roundings looked different. I remember looking
up through the holes in the tent. It looked as if
God had just pushed the stars over and put an

extra one up there just for me. I didn't know what had happened, but I knew that I was happy. There was such a peace and a settledness in my heart—something I had never known.

On the way home I told Rachel that I really wanted her to get saved, too. I also said to Rachel, "I'm going to get up early in the morning and go over and tell Mama and Papa that I got saved."

The next morning I went over to tell Mama and Papa the news. When I got to the house, Mama was churning. I walked into the kitchen and said, "Mama, I got saved last night." She said, "Son, I'm glad." Papa was down in the field hauling watermelons. I walked down to where he was. "Papa," I said, "I got saved last night." Papa looked at me and said, "Tom, you know that Brother Tucker said a man cannot live without sin." Then he got in his wagon and drove off without saying another word. Papa was against us for a long time to come.

The night I got converted I determined that I was going to quit everything that was bad. I thought, "You are supposed to clean up your life when you get saved and sanctified." One thing I could think of to do was to stop smoking. So the next morning when I got up, I threw my pipe out in the yard. I wasn't going to smoke it again. But I wasn't too sure about my chewing tobacco. Could I get along without that—something that had been a part of my life every day since I was six years old?

I put a wad of chewing tobacco in my pocket and carried it around with me, to see if I was going to chew it or not. After three weeks I was going along in the wagon one day, and I threw the chewing tobacco away. It was amazing, but I had never even had a desire to touch it in all that time. I was a changed man.

I PREACH MY FIRST SERMON

I t is hard to explain my first sermon. I sat under a tree and preached to the cows as they grazed in the field. The next sermon I preached was to the posts on the porch. Rachel had gone to Griffin, so I had the house to myself. It's harder to explain why I even thought about preaching. I was bashful and ill-at-ease in public. I had limited education. But preaching was something I seemed to have no choice about. I just knew I had to preach.

My conversion shocked the community. They could see the changes in my behavior. I stopped carrying a gun. I stopped smoking. I went to church every chance I had.

Following the revival, prayer meetings were being held all over the community, and Rachel and I went to every one of them. (Rachel had gotten saved a few nights after I did. I received the baptism of the Holy Ghost in August and Rachel in November.) At one of these prayer meetings after I had been speaking about the Lord, our neighbor, Mr. Kerbow, said, "Tom, will you preach at my house next Sunday?"

This was the second week in September. It was to be my first public sermon. Rachel and I arrived. The house was small, and it was full. People were sitting in the windows. Those who couldn't get into the house filled the yard all the way out underneath the shade trees. People, cars, wagons: they had come to hear the old country boy preach. Some were saying, "He's too mean to make a preacher. He won't last long. It will soon blow over. He will be the laughing stock of the county." But there were others there who stood by me. They believed what I had was real. They said, "The Lord has put His hand on him."

I was so nervous. I knew if I made a mistake old Sister Dean or Brother Abbott or Brother

Malone would know it. Sister Dean was a walking Bible, the godliest woman that lived. Brother Abbott had been preaching for forty years; Brother Malone, for thirty. With these people facing me, I was scared to death.

I had a four-foot space to stand in front of the fireplace in the crowded room. The two preachers and Sister Dean were sitting right in front of me. But when I started my sermon, that was the last sight I had of anybody. I have no idea if I closed my eyes or what; but I never saw Sister Dean or Brother Malone or Brother Abbott again.

I got up before this crowd without anything planned to say. All I had in mind was the text I was going to use to preach. That text was 1 Kings 18:17–21:

> *And it came to pass, when Ahab saw Elijah, that Ahab said unto him, Art thou he that troubleth Israel?*

> *And he answered, I have not troubled Israel; but thou, and thy father's house, in that ye have forsaken the commandments of the Lord, and thou hast followed Baalim.*

> *Now therefore send, and gather to me all Israel unto mount Carmel, and the prophets*

of Baal four hundred and fifty, and the prophets of the groves four hundred, which eat at Jezebel's table.

So Ahab sent unto all the children of Israel, and gathered the prophets together unto mount Carmel.

And Elijah came unto all the people, and said, How long halt ye between two opinions? if the Lord be God, follow him: but if Baal, then follow him. And the people answered him not a word.

I read the Scripture, and then I started to preach. Verse twenty-one was my emphasis: ". . . if the Lord be God, follow Him." For almost an hour I cried against sin and what made man sin in the first place. Then I gave an altar call. People prayed all through the house and out in the yard.

That night old Sister Dean took me over to the side after the service, and she said, "Tommie, I want to tell you something you can count on. Don't ever forget or doubt what I'm about to tell you."

I promised that I wouldn't.

Then she said, "If you will always trust in

God, He will supply all your needs. Put God first, and you will never lack for anything."

I believed her the very moment she spoke. And I've believed her ever since. This has been a creed I've lived by.

Before the evangelist Mamie Akins left the Digby and Brooks community, she talked to Tommie and Rachel at some length and with great fervor about their going to Atlanta to attend the Beulah Heights Bible Institute. Beulah Heights was a small Pentecostal school, with less than fifty students. The school was operated by Sister Hattie Barth and her husband. The program was for two years; it emphasized an in-depth study of the Bible and preparation of the students to preach.

Did Tommie and Rachel want to go? Could they find a way to pay for the cost, if they did want to go? September was a month of questions and decisions.

WE GO TO BIBLE SCHOOL

A fter we got saved, the evangelist, Sister Akins, began to talk to us about going to Bible School in Atlanta. She made it sound so good that we actually thought about going. But school started in October just about the same time as hunting season. I could not make myself believe that Bible School was to take the place of hunting. Why, I had two of the best hunting dogs in the county!

So I made all kinds of excuses not to go to Bible School. But every time I made an excuse, the excuse would fall through. I finally came up with an excuse that I thought was foolproof. I said, "If I can get my crop gathered before school time, then I'll go." Now I knew this was impossible because I hadn't even started gathering anything, and school started in just a few days.

But God was ahead of the plans. The Lord laid it on Mr. Jim Allison's heart to gather all the people in the community who were attending the cottage prayer meetings to come help bring in the crop. There were enough men, wagons, and trucks that came to help that we gathered everything in one day. They pulled the ears of corn off the stalks in the field, loaded it on wagons and trucks, and hauled it into the barn. So there was nothing left to do but go to Bible School. We stored our meager furniture in a vacant room in Rachel's mother's house. Then we left for Beulah Heights Bible Institute on October 15, 1938, to begin the two-year term.

From Fayette County to Atlanta seemed like a long, long trip! We saw no way that we could pay our bill. We were going only on faith. When we arrived in Atlanta, we found the Beulah Heights Bible Institute to be a great place. Sister Hattie Barth and her husband operated the school, which was located in their side yard. They had a large, old, beautiful home, set back among many trees, with a swing and a gazebo in the front yard. It was a very dedicated place— 892 Berne Street in East Atlanta.

The girls were housed upstairs in the Barth home. The boys had small "bunk houses" on the back of the property. Rachel and I had a room in the Barth home on the first floor at the end of the short hall, near the steps that went to the basement. One of my jobs was to keep the furnace heated during the winter months. This helped pay our bill. Later I was made Dean of the boys, and Rachel helped Sister Barth with her private correspondence.

Tending the furnace got me into trouble. The furnace room was right next to the laundry room. The girls used the laundry room every day. We had a rule at the school that men and women could not talk to each other. There was one girl who could not keep the rule when she came down to the laundry room. Her name was Margaret, and she was from Ohio. Whenever I was firing the furnace, she'd stand at the door; and we'd talk. Somebody would always catch us having a conversation and report us. Then Margaret would have to go before Sister Barth, and I'd have to go before Brother Barth. But it was worth it to have some one that would talk to you when you were down there working.

In the dining room were two long tables—the boys sat at one and the girls at one. The girls took turns doing the cooking of the meals. When the Southern girls did the cooking, there was gravy. I would sneak around, with a few more brave boys, to the kitchen door when the girls were cleaning up and sop the pans. We had to keep one eye open for Sister Barth; she was apt to come around most anytime.

As it happens anywhere, even in a Bible School, friction would arise every now and then. Sister Barth was a godly, strict, staid, older woman. She would come to class, make a talk, call a fast, and we had to pray. She'd announce, "There will be no more classes until everything is clean and settled." Such praying we would do, down on the floor, crying and making things right. Students would apologize, hug each other, and ask for forgiveness. No matter how long or how many days it took, we were there until the "air was cleared."

When we went to school, we just walked across the yard. The school had one large room; the different teachers came to us. We had some wonderful teachers. Two were George and Clara Allen. They were especially close to the students, and to Rachel and me in particular. The Allens would go out on weekends preaching, and they would take some students with them most of the time. They would always have many, many religious tracts, and we would throw some out of the car window when we passed someone walking on the road. These were wonderful experiences.

The course of study at Beulah Heights
Bible Institute was, like the rules, rigorous. Tommie and Rachel's texts included Outline Studies in Christian Doctrine, Personal Soulwinning, Dispensational Truth or God's Plan and Purpose in the Ages, *and* Christian Homiletics. *They studied Bibliology: revelation, canonicity, genuineness, authenticity, divine authority, inspiration, ultimate authority. They studied Theology: the character of God, the existence of God, the trinity, attributes, names.*

The course of study also included Anthropology, Hamartialogy (origin of sin, nature of sin); Christology (the person of Christ, incarnation, exaltation); Pneumatology (the Holy Spirit, names, symbols); Ecclesiology (the idea of the Church; government, worship of early Christians); and Eschatology (dispensations, second coming of Christ, resurrection, judgment, closing scenes of time).

The students studied types, symbols, and analogies of the Trinity. They learned in personal soulwinning class how to witness to the self-righteous, the uninterested, the fearful and despairing, the perplexed, the faultfinder and the procrastinator. In homiletics class they learned to do exegesis of the Scriptures.

Most students who attended the Beulah Heights Bible Institute were there because they were preparing to preach; but some, like Rachel, were not preachers but were planning a life of Christian service. Everyone, however, took the same courses. And everyone prepared and delivered sermons, whether or not he or she was planning to preach.

LEARNING TO PREACH

As students in school, you had to preach at least one time a month. You would get up to find a note under your door, telling you where to go to preach. The note might say, "At noon on Saturday go down on Main Street in Atlanta and conduct a street service." It was your responsibility to do everything. You had to find a way to get there and to get any help you could. You had to do the singing if you had any. Then you had to preach like the house was on fire, maybe with no one to listen to you. Sometimes people would gather, and sometimes they would just pass you by. Many times you would walk the two and a half miles back to the school feeling like the whole world was against you. "But it's the making of a preacher," Brother Barth would say. And it proved to be true with many of the boys and girls at the school.

My first assignment was to preach on Decatur Street in Atlanta, and my second assignment was to preach at the Grady Hospital. The day I went to the Grady Hospital, two other boys had the same assignment, but we were to go to different wards to hold our services. None of us talked about what text we were going to use to preach. When we finished preaching and met to go back to the Bible School, I asked one of the other boys, "What did you preach on today?" He replied, "I used John 3:16." The other boy said, "Why, I did, too." I was almost afraid to speak up, thinking they wouldn't believe me; but I said, "I also preached on John 3:16."

It was during that service that I had my

first convert. A Black man had been injured in a sawmill accident. He was in the ward where I was preaching. When I finished, he called me over and said, "I want to tell you that I got converted while you preached." Being the new preacher that I was, I said, "How do you know?" He answered, "I've never felt like this before." I shook his hand, gave him a New Testament, and told him to continue on with his walk in God.

Rachel's first assignment was to go to Alpharetta, Georgia, outside Atlanta. Several of us went with her. She gave a wonderful sermon. She spoke about being in prison, comparing it to people being bound by things other than prison walls. She talked about how the Lord could free us the way He did Peter. Even though she wasn't going to be a preacher, this training came in handy in years to come.

We went strictly on faith at Bible School, and how wonderful it was one day to receive a small check in the mail. We didn't know how it came about, but it was from the United States government—something concerning our farming or planting.

We completed one year of school from October 1938 through May 1939. That summer we went by bus to Mississippi, Alabama, Florida and back to Digby and Brooks preaching revivals, re-modeling churches, and working for the Lord in any way we could.

School began again in the fall of 1939, and we were right there. We were so happy to be back. After Christmas, in January 1940, Papa had a heart attack and was unable to work. I left Bible School and went home to help out. Rachel stayed on until February, the end of the semester. Then she came home. It was a sad time for us, not being able to finish out the final term.

After we got our first church, at Bridgeford, Georgia, we finished paying our school bill. We would travel up to Atlanta in our 1931 Model A Ford. We would put chickens in crates, load up any canned goods we had, such as fruit and vegetables, and take everything up to Sister Barth. She would value the fryers and the canned goods and give us credit on our school bill. So that's how we went to Bible School.

PAPA GETS SAVED

Right before Rachel and I went back to Bible School for our second year, I preached a revival for the Brooks and Digby community. It was in this meeting that Papa got saved. He had fought holiness from the very first. He did not believe that anyone could live a life in God as these people claimed.

I really wanted to see Papa saved. But it looked as if the meeting would close without that happening. I fasted and prayed. My prayer went something like this: "God, I have worshiped my dad. He has been my idol. I have wanted to be like him, which I have done. Now, God, what I want is for him to give his heart to You and become like You, as with Your help I have done."

On Friday night before the meeting was to close on Sunday, it happened. Papa came to the altar—on his own. I went quickly to him and began to pray, putting my arm across his shoulders. Some time later, as we prayed, he raised those big strong arms and cried out, "He has done it! He has done it!"

I said, "What has He done? What?"

He cried, "He has saved me. He has saved me."

The Lord had answered my prayers.

In this meeting several preachers from other churches came trying to get us to join their church. There were two churches that appealed to us: the Pentecostal Holiness Church and the Congregational Holiness Church. But for some reason we went back to Bible School without joining either one of these churches.

Four holiness churches had by the late 1930s developed a significant following in the South: the Fire-Baptized Holiness Church, the Pentecostal Holiness Church, the Church of God in Christ, and the Church of God. All of these churches emphasized the doctrines of sanctification, baptism of the Holy Spirit with speaking in tongues, divine healing, and the second coming of Christ. All of them also emphasized the practice of holiness in daily life. It was the Church of God that Tommie and Rachel Harper were to join.

* * *

In 1886 eight individuals living in the mountains along the Tennessee and North Carolina boundary had joined together to worship in a manner free of man-made traditions and creeds. They chose a name for their organization, the Christian Union. For ten years a minister from this group, R. G. Spurling, Jr., had preached throughout eastern Tennessee and North Carolina the doctrine of the new birth, separation from sin, and holiness. In 1896, the members of the Christian Union moved their services to North Carolina to join with other believers who were also seeking a revival of holiness. It was in services held by this combined group of believers that an outpouring of the Holy Spirit accompanied by speaking in tongues occurred in 1896. Many individuals (estimates range as high as one hundred) received the Baptism of the Holy Spirit during these days of revival, and what would become the Pentecostal movement around the world had begun. (Ten years later similar outpourings would occur in other parts of the United States in places as diverse as Topeka, Kansas, and Los Angeles, California.) In 1902 the worshipers changed their name to the Holiness Church and in 1907 to the Church of God. (The headquarters was established in Cleveland, Tennessee). The Church of God grew from a membership of eight on the day the Christian Union was formed in 1886 to 130 in 1896 to nearly 2,000 by 1911. The growth of the Church of God has been continuous. Recognized today as the oldest Pentecostal denomination in the United States, the Church of God has in 1986 an estimated million and a half members around the world.

*   *   *

When Tommie and Rachel Harper joined the Church of God, the organization was enjoying what has been called "a golden era." The Church of God had grown continuously since its establishment; but beginning in 1928 the Church made outstanding progress. There was a gain of 624 churches between 1928 and 1935, alone. Revivals were held everywhere: under tents, in brush arbors, in vacant schoolhouses, and in homes. The purpose of these revivals was to establish a Church of God in *the community at the end of the meeting. It was one such revival, conducted in a vacant drugstore, which resulted in the establishment of the Church of God in Griffin, Georgia.*

WE FIND A CHURCH

We returned to Bible School in the fall of 1939, but I had to take some weeks off during the fall term to go help Papa on the farm. He cut his foot and almost bled to death, so I went to help pick cotton. Then in January 1940 he had a heart attack, so Rachel and I had to leave Bible School in our last semester and go home to take care of the farm.

During the late summer of 1940 a Brother Powell asked us if we wanted to go with him over to Franklin Springs to a Pentecostal Holiness camp meeting. We rode over there in his car. In the afternoon Rachel and I were sitting in Brother Powell's car, waiting on him to return. On the dash I saw a book. I thought I'd pass the time by reading it.

The book was *The Minutes* of the Church of God. The book contained the teachings and rules for governance of the Church of God. Rachel and I had never heard of this church. And Brother Powell was an ordained minister in the Congregational Holiness Church, so I never did find out why he had a *Minutes* in his car. But as I read the Church's teachings and how the Church operated, I said to Rachel, "This is the church I want to belong to."

I read words like, "The Church of God stands for the whole Bible rightly divided. The New Testament is the only rule for government and discipline." I read the Doctrinal Commitments of The Church of God: repentance, justification, regeneration, new birth, sanctification subsequent to justification, holiness, water baptism, baptism with the Holy Ghost subsequent to cleansing, the speaking in tongues as the Spirit gives utterance, spiritual gifts, divine healing, tithing and giving, and the premillennial second coming of Jesus.

I read the Practical Commitments of the Church: total abstinence from all liquor or strong drinks, against the use of tobacco in any form . . . , that our members dress according to the teachings of the New Testament, against members attending movies, dances and other ungodly amusements, against members swearing. . . .

Yes, this was what I also believed. This was the church that I wanted to belong to.

Much time went by. I was praying and waiting, hoping to find someone who could tell us more about the Church of God. Seven months later, we heard that a Brother P. H. Hammond, a Church of God preacher, had started a revival in an old drugstore near Griffin. It was March of 1941. The weather was cold and bad, but not too cold for Rachel and me to drive fifteen miles in Papa's open-cab Model T truck to attend the meeting. We felt that God had sent this evangelist our way.

From that revival a Church of God was established in Griffin. We were among the first people to join. They didn't know that we'd been waiting since August for an opportunity to become part of this Church—long before we knew a single individual who was a member.

As soon as we joined the Church of God, I began to preach revivals in order to establish new congregations for the Church. I rode the Greyhound Bus to the first revival, in Copperhill, Tennessee. Then Rachel and I went to Griffin and bought a 1931 Model A with big wheels. We paid $125 for the car, $10 down and $12.36 in monthly payments. Then I headed off to preach revivals in south Georgia.

It was May of 1941. That past Christ-mas Day Tommie and Rachel's first child had been born, a daughter they named Elizabeth. The first months of the baby's life had been hard: no milk seemed to agree with her and she had the three-month colic. Now she had pneumonia. Nevertheless, when Tommie was given the opportunity to begin to preach revivals for the Church of God, Rachel urged him to go. She and the baby would join him when Elizabeth was well.

The first revival in Georgia was held in Broxton, a small town approximately 170 miles south of Brooks. The second revival was in Graham, forty miles east of Broxton. The third revival was in Big Oaks and the fourth in Bridgeford, both about ten miles from Graham.

TESTED WITH A TENT

As a new minister of the Church of God, I was asked by the state overseer in Georgia, Reverend A. V. Beaube, to take a tent and hold a meeting in Broxton, Georgia. He wanted a Church of God established there.

The tent was ragged, full of holes. In fact, the canvas was just plain rotten. I went to a dry goods store and bought denim material, the kind Mama made Nonie and me overalls from, and sewed patches on the tent out of this fabric. I had to put up that tent and take it down to patch it three times before we could have service under it.

I went to the mayor of the town to get permission to put the tent on a lot next to the depot. The mayor said, "I'll give you permission to put up your tent if you promise to end the services every night by nine o'clock."

I said, "I can't promise to close the meeting each night by nine o'clock." (You didn't start church back then until dark.)

The mayor said, "Well, there is another lot you can use," and he told me how to find it.

When I found this lot, it was way out of town. The lot had no power at all for lights. "If I put the tent up here," I said to myself, "we will have to use lanterns and flambeaus for light." I got the tent out of the car and stretched it out on the ground; but I just could not put it up so far out of town.

I went over and sat on the front bumper of the car. I was so discouraged. In a few minutes, as I was sitting there staring at the ground and wondering what to do, a little boy came running up.

"I'm hunting a Brother Harper. My grandmother sent him a message."

"I'm Brother Harper," I replied.

"Grandmother said she wants to talk to you."

So I followed the little boy back into town to his grandmother's house.

"I hear you want a place to put your tent up," the lady said to me when I walked up on the porch.

"Yes, M'am, I need a place close into town."

"How about that garden plot right over there?" And she pointed to a big field out to the side of her house.

"That will do nicely," I answered, my heart pumping in my breast.

"Well, it's yours for as long as you want to use it."

So I put up the tent in the lady's garden plot and started having meetings. The revival lasted for three weeks. The crowds grew every night, spilling out of the tent and even out of the garden plot. And it turned out, that garden plot was only 150 yards from the mayor's house. So he got to hear preaching every night for three weeks until long after nine o'clock.

We organized a Church of God at the end.

Brother Beaube told me later that he was testing me with that old ragged tent—to see if I was the stuff a Church of God preacher was made of. I'm glad I passed the test. I guess I should also be glad that I knew how to sew!

THE SHOUTING
POWDER INCIDENT

When I finished the meeting in Broxton, I went back home and got Rachel and the baby. We began the drive back to south Georgia. My driving upset Rachel. She kept saying, "We'll all be dead when we get there." She was constantly accusing me of passing on hills, although I assured her that all we were going to meet was a two-horse wagon or a buggy. I told her we certainly weren't going to meet a car way out here on these south Georgia country roads.

Just before we reached Graham, where our next revival was going to be, Rachel said to me,

"There sure are a lot of little towns down here named the same."

I said, "What are you talking about?"

Rachel replied, "Well, that's about the fifth sign I've seen announcing a town called 'Cattle Crossing.' You'd think folks would get the places mixed up."

I said, "Rachel, those signs are not names of towns. They are warnings to watch out for cows on the road!" We laughed about that for years.

We had church in Graham in an old schoolhouse. The cows had taken the schoolhouse over during the winter to get in out of the bad weather, so Rachel and I had a mess to clean up before we could have church. We cleaned the old building and started our meeting.

The revival was blessed from the beginning. The crowds were great. The power of God touched the hearts of men and women every night. But many people in town still didn't believe in old-time preaching and the kind of services we were having. So somebody started a rumor that the preacher out at the schoolhouse had some powder and that when he sprinkled this powder on people they would shout.

Well, the next night after I heard about the rumor, I tried to defend myself and the Church. I told the congregation, "No, I don't have any such thing as shouting powder. But let me tell you this. If I could find powder that would make people act like this, I'd order a barrelful from Sears Roebuck and pour it on everybody."

The perspiration was running down my face as I talked. So about the time I finished saying, "I'd get a barrel of shouting powder if I could," I pulled my handkerchief out of my back pants' pocket. I slung the handkerchief to get it unfolded and started to wipe my face. When I slung that handkerchief, people jumped out of the building in all directions. Some left through the doors, and some through the open windows. They thought I had shouting powder in that handkerchief and was slinging it all over them.

By the time all the commotion was over, I had almost nobody left to preach to. So I learned never to try to explain about shouting powder again.

GOD SENDS THE BABY MILK

Our baby, Elizabeth, had been sick the first three months after she was born. There was no milk that we could find that would agree with her. She cried night and day. Finally, we found milk she could drink—Carnation evaporated milk. Now she was fine. I really enjoyed having Rachel and her with me in the revivals.

Times were hard that summer of 1941. We had to live in some trying circumstances. Nobody had much money, so the offerings were very slim. I was down to one suit and one dress shirt. Rachel would wash the shirt every day so it would be ready for service that night. It finally got so thin that one night when I was preaching I swung my arms around real big and the shirt split right down the middle. I just turned around and put my coat on and kept preaching.

What really hurt during those times, though, was the baby having to do without. Rachel and I could take about anything, but it was a different matter with our little girl. We did everything we could to keep her healthy and fed.

Finally, though, when we were in a revival in a brush arbor in Big Oaks, we got down to the last can of Carnation milk. Rachel fixed the baby's bottle, and we knew that when that was gone there was no more. We both knew, too, how sick she got with any other kind of milk.

Late that afternoon we got down and prayed. I said, "God, you know we are out doing Your work, preaching to bring souls to the Lord. And you know that we are struggling to make ends meet. You also know this baby is here and that we've just given her her last can of milk. So, God, we're praying for you to supply our needs. You always have, and we know you always will. We are trusting you now."

Then Rachel and I got up off our knees and went on about getting ready for church. We got over to the brush arbor and waited on others to arrive. As it started to get dark, we could see someone coming way across the field, swinging a lighted lantern. When the lady arrived at the brush arbor, we saw that she had her lantern in one hand and a brown paper sack in the other. She handed the sack to Rachel and said, "God laid it on my heart to bring you this." When Rachel opened the sack, it contained one can of Carnation evaporated milk.

I ALMOST GIVE UP

The summer of 1941 I went to my first Church of God camp meeting in Georgia. Rachel and Elizabeth stayed in Brooks, and I drove up to Atlanta every morning and back every night. The camp meeting was held at the Hemphill Avenue Church of God.

No one seemed to care that I was a new man in the Church and knew nobody. I felt so alone. I stood on the lawn of the church and cried.

Driving back down to Brooks after each service, I'd pray, "God, some day let me help young preachers who are in the same circumstance that I am in now to know they are loved and needed in the Church." I got the answer to my prayer as I grew in the Lord and in the Church.

When the camp meeting was over, we were heading back to finish the revival we had started at Bridgeford in south Georgia. Right before we left something happened that brought me the closest to giving up of anything that ever occurred in my spiritual life.

Papa, Nonie, my brother, and I were sitting out on the porch one afternoon. Nonie started telling me how terrible I was. "You don't take care of your family," he said, "You take that little baby off down to south Georgia with no place to live and no money to buy anything. And Rachel has to go without things she needs. What kind of husband and father are you?" I was hurt to the core. But Nonie kept on. He said about the ugliest things anybody could ever say to a brother. I said, "If I wasn't saved, I'd slit your throat." He didn't have any idea how hard it had been for all of us, and he couldn't understand why we did what we did.

Finally, I turned to Papa, who had been sitting there not saying anything. He could tell I wanted him to say something. He just looked at me and said, "You could do better."

Rachel, the baby, and I got in the car to go back to south Georgia. I told Rachel as we were leaving Brooks, "I'm just going to go back to Bridgeford, finish up there, quit preaching, and come back up here and work at Hill's Touchstone Packing House packing peaches.

Rachel was quiet for a minute, and then she said, "God didn't call you to work in a packing house. God called you to preach."

And preach we did. From then until this very day.

OUR FIRST CHURCH
AT BRIDGEFORD

In August of 1941 we were assigned our first church to pastor, the Bridgeford, Georgia, Church of God, where we had run a revival earlier in the summer.

We gathered our few belongings which had been stored in a spare room at Rachel's mother's since we went to Bible School. Mr. Buck Lee moved them for us in his pick up truck. We packed our clothes and gathered up Elizabeth, who now was eight months old. We drove in our 1931 Model A Ford from Brooks to Bridgeford—about 175 miles—to begin a new time in our life.

We were excited. We never wondered if it was the right thing to do. We had already settled that. We had visions of a good country life, doing God's bidding. No matter that the tiny parsonage wasn't quite finished—it had no ceiling and no partitions—and no matter that the tin roof could be cold in winter and scorching in summer. It didn't cross our minds that we had very little money and what would we do? We were going to pastor our first church!

When we got to Bridgeford, we discovered that the church was in bad shape. There were 105 members on the rolls, but the first Sunday we had only six in Sunday School and twelve in the morning service. The next Sunday there were twenty-four in the morning service. This was the attendance for about three months or longer. After a good revival with Sister Mae Terry, however, the church began to grow.

In the Missions Program of the Church of God, each church was called on to raise $3.50 per member. Since we still had 105 members on the books—no matter that probably seventy-five of them could not be found—the Bridgeford Church of God had to raise $367.50. We were a country church, and almost everybody was a farmer. And I knew how little cash farmers had. Every waking hour there was this amount facing us. This was a big load to carry.

We managed to raise $100. Then one member gave a fat steer and bought him back for $60. We had a homecoming and raised another $62.50. This gave us $222.50; there was only $145 left to raise.

By then we could imagine that the church was going to be able to come through with the assessment, and a good spirit prevailed. The church members started selling chickens. We asked for donations from business places in the closest town, Hazlehurst, which was seven miles away. The money kept coming in.

Some members said they would give hogs to raise the rest of the money. So we gathered these hogs up and put them in a pen. I contacted a Mr. Carter from Graham who was a stock buyer. He came over to look at the hogs.

We got out to the pen, and Mr. Carter quoted me a price for the lot. But his offer was $20 short of the amount we had to have.

I said, "Mr. Carter, we need twenty dollars more than that to meet our Missions Program for the Church."

He said, "I've made my offer," and he began to walk away.

I started praying, "God, don't let him leave. Don't let him leave."

He was almost to his truck when he turned around and came back to where I was. He said, "Preacher, you drive a hard bargain. I'm going to give you the extra $20 for these hogs." He loaded the hogs and carried them to the sale barn. He said later that he did not lose any money in the deal. And that was also an answer to prayer. For as he drove off that day, I said, "Oh, God, bless the hogs so that Mr. Carter won't lose any money." Mr. Carter was a special man in the eyes of Tommie Harper. Through him we had made the last $20 of our $367.50 missions pledge.

*   *   *

After we got to Bridgeford and paid the cost of moving, we had less than $200 to live on. We never went wanting; but we sometimes went to the table for dinner, knowing that all we had was a little syrup and no bread.

This was one of those days.

Rachel and I sat down and thanked the Lord for our food as if we had a tableful instead of just one bottle of syrup. Just as we were finishing the prayer, we heard a knock on the porch. Sister Florida Ryles was standing on the ground by the porch. Her arms were full. She said, "While I was praying a few minutes ago, the Lord told me to bring these over to you." She handed us several jars of canned black-eyed peas! To see the Lord work like this gave this young couple faith. (We ate so many peas in those days that I taught the baby a trick. She'd ball up her fist. Then you'd ask her, "What you got in that fist?" And she'd reply, "Ball-bearing peas." People who came to the house thought that was cute.)

There was a time that we were having company for the weekend. We had nothing to fix. We were praying that something would happen so we could have a good dinner. A member of the church came over with five frying chickens. This was more than we had asked for! We had a good Sunday dinner.

Another time we were going to have a visiting preacher. We didn't know what we were going to have for dinner. I had been down in the swamp praying. When I started to go back to the house, I spotted an old bird trap in the hedgerow. I took my knife and cut a trench under the coop. Then I found a nubbin of corn in the field. I shelled the corn and put it in the trench and went on home. Later that day I went back to see if anything had happened. There were fourteen quail in the coop! Again the Lord had answered prayer. Our needs had been supplied.

When I could, I would buy 22 rifle shells

for twenty-five cents a box to use in hunting food for us. I would lie in a fence corner and wait for the doves to come into the field. I would kill enough for dinner and go home happy. Rachel would fix a good meal of birds and gravy and hot biscuits. Again, the Lord had proven that our needs would be taken care of. This we still believe.

Sam Mosley, our neighbor, came over one day. "Preacher," he said, "come out here in the front yard. I want to show you something."

We went out in the yard, and Sam Mosley pointed across the road to his cornfield. "See those rows from here down to that fence? All those are yours. You go gather that corn and trade it to the grocery bus for food." (Every Friday the grocery bus came by; everybody called it the rolling store.) From then on, we traded corn from Sam Mosley's field for sugar, coffee, salt, and meat. Sometimes we'd even have enough to get a mess of fish or some cheese.

* * *

One bad, rainy, wintry night—it was our prayer meeting night—we weren't going to church because we knew the members' custom at times like this. So we were cozy around the wood heater and about to settle in for the night. Then Elizabeth said, "Let's go to church." We tried to explain that people wouldn't be out for church on a night like this; but she kept insisting. She wanted to go to church. So I put my shoes back on and we bundled up and drove the short distance down the road to the church, knowing full well there'd be no one there. But who could deny a baby's pleading to go to church! Sure enough, nobody came but us—so Elizabeth was satisfied to go back home. Later, Rachel wrote her mother about it and Margie replied in her next letter, "A little child shall lead them."

Tommie and Rachel pastored the *church at Bridgeford for three years. In 1944 they were assigned a church seven miles away, in the town of Hazlehurst. Tommie and Rachel did not want to move. The Bridgeford church, after much hard work, was thriving. The Hazlehurst church was floundering. Tommie and Rachel did not want to start over.*

Not only were they being asked to rebuild another church, but Tommie and Rachel were going to have to do so under very different circumstances. Even though the distance between Bridgeford and Hazlehurst was only seven miles, the locations were worlds apart. Bridgeford was a rural community, without even a general store. Hazlehurst was a town of 2500, with banks, government offices, hospitals, and stores. To pastor a church in town, Tommie had to learn how to work with businesses, how to cooperate with agencies and institutions, how to participate in and be an appropriate part of daily civic life.

Making adjustment even more difficult was the fact that the United States was at war. Sugar, tires, and gas were rationed. Loans were hard to get. Money was tight. So for a country boy from Brooks, for whom even living in town was a new experience, pastoring a church in town—and during wartime—was an even greater change. But Tommie and Rachel learned what they had to learn, and God blessed their labors.

Tommie and Rachel also had another child. In 1945, five days before Christmas, a beautiful daughter was born. They named her Barbara Allen.

THE MOVE TO HAZLEHURST

We were enjoying the church at Bridgeford. The church was taking good care of us. We loved the people and were doing a good work. Then, in 1944, the state overseer assigned us to the Church of God at Hazlehurst.

The church was in bad shape. There were no services during the week. Sunday School was held once or twice a month. The tithes averaged

$29 a month for the year, and the church had no parsonage.

Rachel and I could not believe that we were being asked to leave a church we had worked so hard to build up—and had been so successful at—to go to a church in the shape the Hazlehurst church was in. It seemed so unfair.

When I got to the General Assembly in Birmingham, I saw the overseer almost as soon as I walked into the auditorium. He called out, "Here's my Georgia preacher who's going to Hazlehurst."

I said, "That's what I want to talk to you about."

He answered, "You're going. Yes, you're going; and you're going to turn out that man that's running the church."

And that was that.

This was the first and last time Rachel ever talked back to an overseer. She blurted out, "Are you going to starve us to death?" The overseer told her, "You'll make it." And make it we did. But I had to pray through three times before going to that church. (When the overseer came to Hazlehurst a year or so later to preach us a revival, he, Rachel, and I looked back at that time and laughed. But it was no laughing matter when it happened.)

We moved to Hazlehurst, into a duplex with a Mrs. Christian. When we first arrived, life for a Church of God preacher and his wife was very hard. The townspeople in Hazlehurst did not like the Church of God. I found this out the first day I went to the grocery store. I got what I needed and went up to the counter. The man who owned the store ignored me. He waited on several other people who came to the counter after me before he finally waited on me. (I had been identified to him as the new preacher at the Church of God.) This happened a time or two.

The next time I went into the grocery store, I got what I needed and went up to the counter. The owner ignored me again. I had had all I was going to take. When the man started to wait on other people who had come up after me, I spoke up and said, "I'm next."

The owner said, "You don't have to be."

I replied, "If you don't take my money for these things, I'll walk out of this store with this picnic ham and this bottle of syrup."

The owner took my money, and things were fine from then on.

I also had to learn to hold my own at the bank when I had to appear before the bank president who was in charge of ration books during the war. I had a B ration book which allowed me only thirty gallons of gas for a month. This had been plenty in Bridgeford, but now I used more gas since I had to drive more in town. I was also District Overseer of the Hazlehurst District. This meant there were five other churches and pastors that I had to visit and assist when they needed help—over in places like Lumber City, West Green, Denton, and Big Oaks.

I applied to the Ration Committee on Gas for an A book, which would give me sixty gallons of gas a month. I also applied to them for one new tire. (There was no spare on the Model A.) I went down to the bank to appear before the committee. The bank president, who was head of the committee, brushed me off. "Oh, your ration book will be in the mail tomorrow." I waited . . . the next day and then the next . . . until six days had passed. There was no ration book in the mail.

So I went back down to the bank. "I want to apply for an A ration book and one new tire," I repeated. This time the bank president was hateful and stern. No, I would not get an A book, and I would not get a new tire. And that was that.

I decided I would appeal to the regional committee in Savannah. I called and learned that they were to be in Hazlehurst on a certain day. I went to the bank to see them. When I arrived, I was totally surprised. The regional committee wasn't there yet, but the bank president said to me, "Come on in, Preacher. I've found out two things about you: You are not a member of that Harper family over in Denton who are conscientious objectors, and you are going to do whatever you have to do to look after your members and that church. I'm going to see that you get what you need."

From that day on Colonel Rogers was a friend. When we were finished, he walked with me to the door of the bank. It was right before Christmas. As I started to leave, Colonel Rogers said, "Preacher, here's something for you and your family for Christmas." He reached into his pocket and pulled out two twenty dollar bills.

* * *

One of the families in the church was on welfare. Even though they got only a small amount of money each month, they paid tithes. When the lady who ran the welfare office found out that this family gave ten percent of their money to the church every month, she got very mad.

"Nobody who gets welfare from Jeff Davis County Relief Board is going to give the taxpayer's money to a church," she snapped. "Your welfare check is cut off, as of today."

The family came to me. I prayed about what to do. Finally, I decided, "I'm going to find out where Judge Knox lives, and I'm going over there and talk to him about this situation." But another voice said, "You can't just up and go over to a judge's house. He doesn't know you, and you probably have no right to go talk to him anyway." But I had to do something about this outrage.

So I found out where Judge Knox lived, and I went over to his house. I knocked on the door, and his wife said that he wasn't home. "He's across the street, visiting the Methodist preacher in his office," she said. So I headed on across the street. I found the office on the second floor of the Methodist church, and I went in. Judge Knox was there.

"Judge Knox," I said, "I've come to talk with you about some members of my church who have had their welfare check cut off. I'm pastor of the Hazlehurst Church of God."

"Oh, I know who you are," the Judge said, "I

hear you every Sunday night. Colonel Rogers and I sit outside your church in the car and listen to you preach."

The next day the family was reinstated on the welfare rolls. I knew then that people in town had begun to take notice of the Church of God. We had gained their respect. When I'd go down to the hospital to visit the sick, I would often run into Dr. Yoman at somebody's bedside. Dr. Yoman would say to the patient, "You call for Reverend Harper and for me, and we'll get you healed. He'll pray for you, and I'll give you the medicine." It was a partnership that was hard to beat!

* * *

It was March of 1945. We had been pastoring the Hazlehurst church for a few months. One Sunday night while we were having service, a stranger came running in from the side door up to the rostrum where I was preaching. He whispered in my ear. I turned to the congregation and said, "We must dismiss church. The house where Rachel and I live is burning." Everybody in the church went over to see if anything could be done.

When we arrived, the fire truck was already there, putting water on the house. But it was no use; the entire thing was in flames. The firemen couldn't even get close to the house; the heat was blistering. Driving up, I had hoped I could get inside and save a few of our things. But all I could do was join everybody else—and it looked as if the whole town was there—standing outside watching the house burn to the ground.

Rachel and I got over to the side of the crowd a little bit and just stood there, watching the flames. I had Elizabeth in my arms. Person after person—many of them we did not even know—came over to say how sorry they were about our loss. Several of them hugged Elizabeth's legs.

The next day when the ashes cooled, Rachel and I went over to the house and sifted through the debris. We hoped we could find some of the coins from the Sunday School offering which we had taken home the day the house burned. We were able to find only about thirty-eight cents. We put that in a pint jar to keep until we could deposit it in the bank. Rachel also found some twisted forks and spoons. We tried to straighten them, but they had melted beyond repair.

Right before we started to leave, Rachel

said, "Tommie, look. Here's my engagement ring." (Rachel hadn't worn her rings since we joined the Church of God; but they meant a lot to her and she kept them in a little pocketbook in the dresser drawer along with other keepsakes from the past.) I took my knife and scraped off some of the soot that had baked onto the ring, and we put it in a handkerchief to take home.

We also found Elizabeth's baby rocking chair. It was burned, but you could still recognize what it was. At four years old, she was too big to sit in it now. But we treasured the chair. I told Rachel, "Let's take it with us. I think I can cut some wood and repair it." So we took the chair.

This event brought people into our lives that we would never have met. The town came together with clothes, furnishings, everything we needed. Businessmen in town helped me build a parsonage. A Mr. Usury gave the lumber which was sawmill rough. Then a man that owned a planing mill with kilns to dry lumber came by, saw the wood, and said, "You can't build a house with rough lumber." He sent his truck, picked up the lumber, carried it down to his mill, dried it, planed it, and brought it back. We then built a nice four-room parsonage.

*   *   *

We were delighted when our new daughter, Barbara, was born the next December. As she grew, she loved to go to church just like her big sister. Sister Ann Brown would come down from Atlanta to preach us a revival, and she'd always go over to the church to pray during the day. Barbara was just barely walking, but she'd hear Sister Brown in the church. She'd toddle over there, crawl up the steps, and go inside.

Sister Brown would be down in the altar praying. Barbara would head straight for the piano. She'd reach her hands up to the keys, and she'd bang on them as hard as she could. The sudden loud noise would scare Sister Brown almost to death. She never got used to Barbara slipping into the church, which she did just about every time Sister Brown went over there. But Sister Brown loved that Barbara. They were buddies from the very start.

* * *

One sad event happened while we lived in Hazlehurst. We sold the old faithful Model A and bought a new '47 Ford. You may say, "Why sad?" After all, we were buying a new car! To us, however, the Model A seemed almost like a member of our family. It had carried Rachel, Elizabeth, and me—and even Barbara for the while she had been born—many, many miles. We treasured that car. It had been used in God's work since we bought it in 1941. When the man who bought the car drove it away, Rachel stood out in the street and cried.

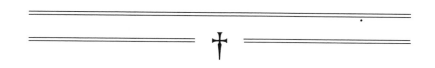

Tommie with his horse.

Tommie home from Michigan.

Tommie and Rachel at Bible School.

Tommie, Rachel, and Elizabeth.

Elizabeth in front of parsonage at Bridgeford.

Tommie at Hazlehurst.

Rachel at Hazlehurst.

Barbara and Elizabeth.

PART
III

SERVICE
1948–1974

. . . the Lord was my stay. He brought me forth also into a large place. . . .

Psalms 18:18–19

Tommie and Rachel pastored the

Hazlehurst Church of God for approximately three and a half years. During that time, the church grew from a Sunday attendance of twenty or thirty to more than a hundred. The tithes increased from $29 a month to an average of $400 to $500. A new parsonage was built.

The other five Churches of God on the Hazlehurst District prospered also. A newspaper article published in the late summer of 1947 and written by Miss Hope Jordan, a keen observer and strong supporter of the Hazlehurst Church of God although not a member, gives this account:

"I was glad when they said unto me, let us go into the house of the Lord." Psalm 122:1 The state convention of the Churches of God in Georgia closed Sunday, July 8, with the record of being one of the best conventions in years. The fine messages were enjoyed by everyone attending the convention, and there was the feeling of united strength amongst the ministers of the state. After the spiritual feast, there were the reports from the twenty-one districts of the state. Each district overseer had a wonderful report to make on his respective district.

Reverend Tommie Harper, pastor of the Hazlehurst Church of God, and district overseer of the Hazlehurst district, was glad to make his report of how God had blessed this district by each of the six churches making a gain.

Reverend Harper is glad to have on his district the church that raised the most mission offering per capita, with $6.83 per member average, than any other church over the entire state. Reverend J. A. Clements, pastor of the Big Oaks Church of God, made this fine record.

The six churches in this district have raised this year for missions, orphanage, old-age ministers, and improvements on property the amount of $3,913.31. We are giving God the praise for all and wish to thank you friends of the church that have helped us accomplish this good work for the Lord. We feel encouraged to press the battle for God and the right, and we need your prayers and continued cooperation.

Hope Jordan, Church Reporter

It was now January 1948. The pastor of one of the largest Churches of God in Georgia was moving to take another assignment. Tommie, who had preached a revival at this church earlier, was elected by the membership to be the new pastor. The state overseer concurred and appointed Tommie Harper pastor of the Rossville, Georgia, Church of God. The Harper family was moving north. To the farthest northwest corner of the state, to the last city in which you could live and still have a Georgia address.

It was a big move: from a town of 2500 to a metropolitan area of 213,000. From a district of six churches to a district of thirteen. From a church with a hundred members to a church with several hundred. From a congregation which was a mixture of country and town to a congregation that was urban. Once again, Tommie and Rachel would have a lot to learn.

WE MOVE ON

When we moved to Rossville the last of January 1948, it was cold, cold. Rossville was a much larger church than the one we had left, but we were eagerly looking forward to meeting new friends and doing our best for God and lost souls. They greeted us with open arms and received us graciously.

We had two bedrooms in the small parsonage, but we chose to keep our girls near us.

So each night we would bring in the rollaway bed and put it against our bed. Our seven-year-old and our two-year-old would nestle together. The next morning we would close the rollaway bed up and roll it back out on the closed-in back porch.

We enrolled Elizabeth in the second grade, and Barbara went with us on visitation. When we visited our people in the hospital, she would have to stay in the lobby. We placed her in a chair right in front of the elevator; and, after telling her not to move, we went up to the sick rooms. When we came back down, she would be right there!

The twelve and a half years at Rossville were happy ones. A wonderful event in our personal lives occurred while we lived there. Our son, Frank, was born. Rachel and I were overjoyed, and the girls were thrilled. They would argue over who would get to take care of him. Later, when he was older, they argued over who had to take care of him! Frank finished the first grade while we were at Rossville; Barbara entered school and graduated from junior high; and Elizabeth went from the second grade through high school and entered college. Rossville became the Harpers' home, and the Rossville church members became the Harpers' family.

The demands of ministering to sev-
eral hundred church members, of administering governance and spiritual leadership for thirteen pastors and
their churches on the Rossville District, and of carrying
out the civic and social responsibilities that came with
pastoring in a big city required deep wisdom and en-
larged compassion. Tommie was required to broaden the
scope of his work.

The ministry of the Rossville Church of God did
increase to include a new bus to bring people in for services, an Off-the-Street Club to clothe, feed, and minister
to children and young people in need, and an interdenominational, city-wide storehouse which distributed
food and clothing to the needy. (The Rossville Church of
God initiated the establishment of the storehouse which
was administered by the Greater Chattanooga Area Ministerial Council.) The Rossville Church of God also had a
radio broadcast which was heard in a wide regional
area. Somehow God managed to transform a country
boy into an urban minister.

But in all the growth, Tommie Harper remained
Tommie. God worked through the man as he was. This
meant that the solutions to problems were often unusual.

GOD, KILL HIM.
KILL HIM RIGHT NOW

Although I had been district overseer at Hazlehurst, that district was smaller than the Rossville District. Now I was kept busy taking care of my own church and serving the twelve other churches on the district. I visited these churches at least every quarter and more often if trouble arose.

One of the churches on the district had been in trouble so often that it became known as the problem church which no one wanted to pastor. I would go out and get things working again, and before I would get back home the members would be at each other's throats.

I became outdone with the whole church. So I came up with a solution. I decided that the best thing to do was to disband the whole church and turn out all the members as troublemakers who were sowing discord. I called a meeting at that church. When I opened the meeting, I said, "Tonight I'm disbanding this church, and I'm turning out every member." Then I proceeded to take every member's name off the church roll. The people were shocked.

After I got through disbanding the church, I read the Church of God *Minutes*. I said, "I am now going to organize a new church. This church will have as its members only those of you who are willing to accept and live by the teachings of the Church of God. Anybody who wants to be a part of this new church is welcome to come up and join." Well, even if the solution to the problem was different, it got rid of the troublemakers, and a church was set in order with all new members. Then a new pastor was appointed, and the church went to work and had a good year.

* * *

I would preach revivals as much as I could while we were pastoring Rossville. Once I was preaching a revival under a big tent for the Trenton, Georgia, church. The tent was crowded each night.

One Friday night as I was preaching, a young man came running into the tent. This frightened the congregation. I stopped preaching, walked down, and met the young man.

I asked him, "Why are you disturbing this meeting?"

He said, "I want to get saved."

So I led him to the altar and called the people up to pray with him, which they did with all honesty of spirit.

I walked back to the front of the tent while the people were praying, and there was a policeman. "That boy ran in here to get away from the law," the policeman said.

I told the officer, "Go around to the back of the tent and wait. The fellow will try to sneak out while the people are praying."

Sure enough, this happened. While he thought people weren't looking, the boy began to crawl out backwards. What he didn't know was that the policeman was standing there, waiting for him.

As the boy was slipping out from under the tent, the officer caught him by the legs. The boy caught the tent curtain and wouldn't let go. A big struggle went on. It looked as if the boy was going to pull that tent to the ground before it was over. The policeman finally got the boy loose from the tent and took him away.

After things quieted down, I went ahead and finished my sermon. Later it was told around town: "If you get in trouble with the law, don't go around that tent. If you come in the front, the preacher will push you out the back—right into the hands of the police!"

* * *

There was this fellow who came to the Rossville church who would get saved in every revival. Then he'd backslide before the next one. Sometimes he'd even backslide before the revival was over. Well, another revival was going on and this man got saved again.

I was down praying with him the night he got reconverted. When the man prayed through, he started shouting for joy. I immediately put my hands on his shoulders and began to pray, "God, kill him. Kill him right now." The man became greatly disturbed listening to me asking God to kill him.

He stopped praying and said, "Preacher, why in the world are you praying for God to kill me?"

I answered, "Well, if you leave this altar, you will backslide before the meeting is over. It will be much better for you to die and go to heaven right now than to take the chance of losing out with God." And I started praying again, as loudly as I could, "God, kill him. Kill him right now."

The fellow said, "Help me. I don't want to go to hell." He got serious with the Lord. And now thirty years later he is still saved and has been a good worker in the church all these years.

The Rossville church grew and pros-pered. The national publication of the Church of God, the Evangel, *had as its cover picture and story on April 2, 1956, the Rossville, Georgia, Church of God. The article was written by Gladiola Polivka, the church reporter. An excerpt follows:*

> "We would like to sound a note of praise from the Rossville Church of God for all the wonderful blessings of the Lord. . . . Brother Tommie Harper came to us as pastor eight years ago (January 1948). . . . Since 1948, the church has gained in every department and has broken its previous records while establishing many new records. . . .
> The Lord blessed, and we soon realized that we were not able to take care of the people as they came. We then began to look for ways to meet the demands that were facing the church. As there was no way for us to expand in our present location, we began scouting to find a new location.
> In 1951, we purchased three lots at 309 Andrews Street, Rossville, which included a 12-room house. This was purchased for $13,500 and in April, 1951, the pastor and family moved into the new parsonage. The Lord blessed, and the church was able to pay our debt in 18 months. We then started our

plans for a new church. This seemed to be an impossibility at that time because of buying restrictions on materials. However, after much prayer, fasting and work by the pastor and faithful loyal members as well as our good friends and business acquaintances, the Lord blessed us with a beautiful brick edifice that is now known as the Rossville Church of God. On Mother Day's, 1954, we had our dedication. . . .

Recently, the church bought three additional lots below the church which gives it a full block and brings our value on the parsonage and church property to $95,480. We truly praise God for all the progress made. . . ."

During the 1950s much turmoil and spiritual upheaval occurred in the Chattanooga area. Tommie Harper took a stand early against the practices he believed were not of God. At times this stand was unpopular. At times his motives were questioned. At times he was criticized for being stubborn, mean, and hard. It was a period of uncertainty, disturbance, and unrest.

THE OUTCOME
OF THE WILDFIRE

Everything was going well with us at the Rossville church. Then suddenly trouble began.

A young man had started preaching in Atlanta and had become a sensation overnight. An established Church of God preacher brought this young man to Chattanooga to introduce him to pastors in our area. Right away the young evangelist began to preach at one of our largest Churches of God.

Well, the truth is that he didn't preach so much as he prayed for the sick. For his was a healing ministry. After the song service was over, the pastor of the church would announce, "Here is God's man for God's hour." And with a flourish this young evangelist, dressed always in a shiny white suit, would emerge from a room at the back of the platform.

His service always centered around praying for the sick. People would line up two or three deep to be prayed for by this young preacher. The young man would go up and down the lines, stopping in front of each person to pray. He would touch the people on the forehead and immediately they would fall to the floor, knocked out by the power of God. This was such a regular occurrence that the young evangelist stationed assistants with a white cloth draped over their arms behind each person. These assistants were waiting to cover the people when they fell to the floor. Many miracles were reported, and the news spread far and wide.

I suspected this activity from the very first. But it was a difficult thing. If people really were being saved and healed, how could I doubt what was going on? Members from my church flocked to the healing services by the scores. So did the members of all the other pastors' churches in the area.

A few weeks after this revival began (it ran for two months or longer), several of us pastors who were in the Greater Chattanooga Ministerial Association went up to Cleveland to meet with the officials of the Church. We wanted them to know what was happening in Chattanooga and that we were worried. After we gave our report, one of the executives said, "Well, men, I think you may just be a little bit jealous." And that was the end of that. I went home questioning: was the problem in me?

We ministers didn't know what to do. We met together. The first question we had to ask ourselves was whether or not we were the ones who were wrong. Perhaps this young man was especially touched by God. Perhaps we just weren't open to see it. Several of the ministers said, "We'll go join the prayer line. If this man is of God, we'll know it when we are prayed for." So they did. The result was that after being "touched" by the young evangelist, each pastor reported that he had been pushed to the floor by the pressure exerted on his forehead. With that information the Ministerial Association filed charges with the Church of God officials against the evangelist. The charges included dishonesty and sowing discord, among other things.

This broke the whole thing wide open. The pastor of the church where the young man preached said he would leave the Church of God before he would betray the evangelist. And he did. The pastor resigned as a minister in the Church of God and established his own independent church. Hundreds of Church of God members left their own congregations and joined the independent church. Twenty-nine of the families in the Rossville church—good people, people who had been established for decades in the Church—joined the independent church. You almost needed daily bulletins, as in wartime, to keep up with all that was going on. There was total upheaval. We ministers were criticized on every hand.

This was one of my hardest times. I had to spend hours and days in prayer. I fasted for weeks at a time. My flock was being torn up. Many of my people were being led astray. People were giving money left and right; some of my members even mortgaged their homes and cars to finance this new church. One of the old men in my church, probably in his eighties, while his wife was in the hospital, took the family radio to give to the pastor of the independent church. He wanted to do what he could to help. That broke my heart. And what made matters even worse was that I kept asking myself: are we ministers wrong?

As the weeks went on, however, through prayer and fasting, I came to know what was right. I did not care what anybody said about me from that time on. I was going to stand for God and the Church, no matter what.

* * *

One Saturday afternoon I got a telephone call. The lady on the other end was one of the people who had left the Rossville church and joined the independent group. When I answered the phone, she said, with a sneer in her voice, "Well, do you know what happened last night? Old Sister Simpson got healed! Now I guess you won't have anything else to say."

Sister Simpson, who was probably in her seventies, had been blind for years. She got around by holding onto her husband's arm when they walked.

The caller had asked me, "Aren't you going down to her house to see her? To see this miracle that has occurred?"

I answered, "No, I'm not going. If she can see today, she'll be able to see tomorrow. So I'll just wait to see her at church."

The next morning I went outside and headed across the street to the church for Sunday School. I looked down to my right, and here came old Brother and Sister Simpson walking up the road. She was leaning on his arm. She could not see. I was so sad for these good people and the hundreds like them who were seeking what they were not going to find.

* * *

The situation got worse before it got better. After the young evangelist left town, other individuals and groups passed through Chattanooga, appearing at the independent church for some period of time. There was the woman with diamonds and rubies in her teeth. Night after night she'd stand on the rostrum of the independent church and let the congregation come up to look into her mouth. They came to see the teeth that God had filled with jewels!

There was also the young teen-ager with the plastic eye.

"Come see the man who can read with a plastic eye," the word went out. Crowds came. Hadn't an eye doctor confirmed this miracle? The young man could read a chart laid on his chest; he could read it with his plastic eye.

I almost got into serious trouble over this plastic eye. It happened like this:

One Sunday morning I suggested to my congregation that perhaps this young man was reading this chart with his good eye, not his plastic eye, and that it might be good to wait until further confirmation came in, before giving God the credit for the miracle.

I was president of the Greater Chattanooga Ministerial Association at this time, and we pastors had decided to hold a city-wide union revival. We hoped by this to bridge over the situation so that all would not be lost, and we hoped to build up a standard of worship worthy of the Church of God. Reverend Ray H. Hughes was the speaker, and all of the ministers in the Churches of God in the Chattanooga area were participating.

On Sunday afternoon, after I had made the recommendation to my congregation about the plastic eye, I was standing on the platform at the tent revival, waiting for the service to begin. Suddenly a woman came charging at me and shoved me as hard as she could. She was trying to push me off the rostrum to the ground below, a drop of probably six or eight feet.

"What do you mean," she screamed, "saying my boy is reading out of his good eye? He sees out of his plastic eye. And don't you say anything else!"

I barely managed to get my balance before I fell off the platform. I had been attacked by the mother of the boy with the plastic eye.

"Oh, the perils of being a Church of God preacher," the other ministers kidded me later. But we all knew that the situation, while on occasion something we had to laugh about, was a very serious matter.

Finally the wildfire burned out. It took about seven years. The independent church went bankrupt. Good people lost their mortgaged homes and cars. The large "temple" which the independent preacher had built became first a furniture store and then later a movie theater. The young evangelist in the white suit never returned to Chattanooga to preach again. The lady with the diamonds and rubies in her teeth got arrested by the FBI in another city, charged with fraud. The teen-ager reading with the plastic eye turned out to be a hoax. In the end the Churches of God in Chattanooga were stronger than they had ever been. God rewarded us with congregations of dedicated men and women whose purpose was to follow Christ. We had passed through the fire.

In the Bible which Tommie Harper *used to preach from during these turbulent years can still be found a small, worn piece of paper. On this piece of paper he had written:*

Men of prayer.

Charles Simeon prayed from four till light in the morning.

Wesley spent two hours daily in prayer.

John Fletcher stained the walls of his room by the breath of his prayers.

Luther said, "If I fail to spend two hours in prayer, the devil gets the victory through the day."

John Welch thought the day ill-spent if he did not spend eight to ten hours in prayer. His wife would complain when she found him lying on the ground weeping. "O, woman, I have the souls of 3000 to answer for and I know not how it is with many of them."

One of the members of the Rossville church became disillusioned and discouraged during the time of religious upheaval. He later reported this event:

There was a time that I got disheartened and quit going to church for about three months. I had saved my tithes for this period of time and put them in an envelope.

I got up one morning, and no one knew what I was going to do. I sat down and wrote a letter to Brother Harper, telling him of my decision. My intention was to come out of the church, so I asked in the note to have my name taken off the books. I put this note in another envelope. I put the two envelopes, the one containing the tithes and the one containing my note, in my coat pocket.

Not calling before I left, I went over to the parsonage to talk to Brother Harper. I stepped on the back porch and knocked on the door. Sister Harper came to the door and greeted me as only Sister Harper can—the sweetest voice a person ever heard.

I asked to see Brother Harper, and Sister Harper said, "Brother Oliver, Tommie's downstairs praying for you right now. He is waiting for you to come over. Go on down to the office."

I said, "Sister Harper, he doesn't know that I am coming over here. Nobody knew I was. So how can he be waiting on me?"

"Why, Brother Oliver, I don't know. But he's been down there praying for you for quite a while. He knew you were coming. Go on downstairs and see him," she said.

As I went downstairs, I wondered, "How in the world did he know I was coming?" I knocked on the door, and Brother Harper answered.

As soon as I stepped into the room, he said, "Brother Oliver, one of the envelopes that you have in your pocket I will take. The other one you keep in your pocket until we have prayed about it."

I said, "Brother Harper, how did you know what I've got in my pockets?" He told me the Lord had already spoken to him about it. I'll tell you, right then I got on my knees and I prayed through to victory. Brother Harper taught me a lesson that morning. I know it was God through Brother Harper, but it worked. I knew that God had been talking to this man and, better still, this man had been talking to God.

One of the things Tommie Harper enjoyed most during his days at the Rossville church was conducting the weekly radio broadcast, The Shut-In Hour. It was a far cry from those early days on the homeplace when the whole community would gather round the new gray Gramophone with the big handle and listen to songs like "That Ole Daddy of Mine," "Lone Pine Tree,"

*and "When the Moon Comes Over the Mountain."
There'd be no sound back then as everybody sat listening. No sound except the spitting of chewing tobacco by
the men and the swish of black gum brushes from the
women as they put snuff in the back of their mouths. But
perhaps it was not such a far cry after all. Perhaps that is
where Tommie got his first glimpse of how drawing and
compelling communication by distance could be.*

*At any rate, he loved the radio broadcast. He en-
joyed having people show up at church who had heard
the service on the air. He was moved when people wrote
him about being saved and healed while they listened.
And over the years the broadcasting range of the radio
station WDXB increased. Tommie wondered just how far
the program was heard.*

HOW TALL IS BROTHER HARPER?

We had a radio broadcast the entire
time I pastored the Rossville church. It was called
the Shut-In Hour. Many people would come to
church who had heard the radio program from
as much as seventy-five miles away. I decided to
find out just how far the Shut-In Hour was heard,
so I started a write-in program. The person writ-

ing a letter postmarked from the farthest away would be given a New Testament; and if the writer could describe Brother Harper in size and height, he or she would get a complete Bible.

Well, a letter came in from Florida! Now there was no way the broadcast could be heard way down there. But the letter contained a perfect likeness of Brother Harper: six feet two, 220 pounds, black hair, brown eyes. We could not understand how this man, unknown to us and living way down in De Land, Florida, could know who Tommie Harper was. I sent him the Bible anyway. That letter was a surprise and a puzzle for a long time.

Finally, the next summer at the Georgia Camp Meeting the puzzle was solved. An evangelist who had been with us in a revival and had known about this campaign had told a pastor in Florida Tommie Harper's size and weight. This pastor was the one who had written the letter. The evangelist came up to me at camp meeting and told me about the letter. He apologized for the trick; but he said, "Brother Harper, that preacher in Florida really needed a new Bible!"

It was at that same camp meeting that the state overseer, Brother E. L. Simmons, came to me and said, "Brother Harper, the strangest thing has happened. Thirteen different preachers have come up to me during this camp meeting and reported that the Lord has laid it on their hearts to go to the Rossville church to pastor."

I looked at the overseer for a minute, and then I said, "Well, Brother Simmons, I know the fourteenth. And he's going to stay!"

A PREACHER NEVER
SUCCEEDS ALONE

During the days of pastoring at Rossville, there were times when I could not be at home at night. The Georgia State Council might be meeting, or I might be away working at Youth Camp or running a revival. Rachel stood by to carry on the work at home and at the church. Even though she wasn't a preacher, she would give a little talk at prayer meeting if I had to be away, using the skills we learned in our homiletics class in Bible School.

I remember once she prepared a message on "Bones." She talked about wish bones (people in the church always wishing for things to get better but doing nothing about them), jaw bones (people in the church always complaining, telling how it ought to be done), and back bones (people in the church who did whatever work was to be done, always being there, always being dependable). Another time her talk was on the word WATCH. She said, "In order to live the life of a Christian, we must watch our: W . . . words; A . . . actions; T . . . thoughts; C . . . companions and keep H . . . heaven in view!

The congregation always liked it when Rachel gave the message, although she was quick to report that she wasn't a preacher. She was just filling in.

Even when I was in town, I had to be gone from home almost all day every day. Rachel went with me as much as she could to visit the sick and help our members; but especially after Frank was born she was the one who stayed at the house to take care of the home front. There were the children to take care of, messages to get when the telephone rang, the house to clean, meals to cook, members to talk with—it was more than a full-time job.

And Rachel was the best. I give credit to her and say there was no one better in the role of a pastor's wife. She did a good job of raising the family, too. She was often left with the task of disciplining the children. Most of the time, she administered the discipline herself. But I remember one time that she left the correction to me.

Frank had got into some of my books, which he had been trained not to do, and had made marks all over them. Rachel told him, "I'm going to wait and tell your Daddy when he gets home and let him take care of you."

When I came home and sat down in my chair, Frank, who was about four, came running in and jumped into my lap. He hugged my neck and said, "Daddy, I love you."

In reply, I said, "I love you, too."

He hugged me again real hard and said, "I love you. I love you."

The third time he hugged me real hard and said, "I love you, I love you, I love you."

I replied, "I love you, I love you, I love you," and hugged him back real hard.

Frank then looked at Rachel and said, "Now, tell him!"

As you might guess, there could never be a whipping at a time like that.

In 1960 Tommie Harper was promoted

to the position of state overseer. This meant that he would no longer pastor a church but would, instead, be in charge of all the Churches of God in a certain state. The appointment was to Washington, which was known as a "mission state." This meant that the finances were not sufficient to support the work in the state. Supplementary assistance had to come from the General Headquarters of the Church of God.

Washington state covered 66,511 square miles. There were twenty Churches of God in the state, scattered from the Strait of Juan de Fuca to Pasco, Longview, and Kennewick. Since the overseer's job was to nurture, build up, and minister to the churches and their pastors in the state, he had to do extensive traveling. By the time the four-year appointment to Washington was completed, Tommie had put 130,000 miles on one car and 119,000 on another.

The state overseer's job also included managing the business affairs of the Church's operation in the state. This meant budgets, accounting and filing systems, special reports, loans, repayment schedules, legal matters, and a large volume of correspondence between the State Office and the pastors and the State Office and the General Headquarters in Cleveland, Tennessee. Again, Tommie and Rachel had much to learn.

Becoming a state overseer also meant that for the first time since 1941 Tommie and Rachel had no church to whom they were pastor and family. And while they were made welcome and treated graciously at all the churches they visited, there was no flock to whom they belonged. Added to this were other concerns: the long distance between Washington state and Georgia, the difference between the cultures of the two sections of the country, the absence of one member of the family who *had remained behind. Without question, the Harpers faced challenging adjustments.*

NORTHWEST, HERE WE COME

The year was 1960. We had just received our seventh appointment back to the Rossville church, with a vote of ninety-seven percent of the membership. We would be pastoring there two more years. Things were looking good. We were happy and thrilled to be going back.

That year at the General Assembly in Dallas, Texas, we were in the audience when the names were read off for the position of state overseer. Suddenly, I heard my name: Tommie Harper— Washington. I had been appointed the overseer of Washington state! This was a great surprise; I had never dreamed of going out as a state overseer. No one had even given a hint that this might happen.

We went home with a confused mind. The appointment meant we would have to leave our little nest in Rossville and move over 3,000 miles to the West Coast. And we'd have to do this in one week's time. We'd have one last Sunday at the Rossville church.

*   *   *

The big moving van pulled in, loaded our household goods, and pulled out. We loaded the car and made ready to leave. This was the hardest thing as a family we had ever faced. Our oldest daughter Elizabeth had to be left behind to finish her college education. With the other two children, Barbara and Frank, we headed out for the long trip west.

After making the cross-country trip of almost 3,000 miles from Georgia to Washington and being on the road about four days and three nights, we arrived at our new home—616 North 10th Avenue, Yakima, Washington. We were filled with great anticipation. Some of the ministers and their wives welcomed us and supplied us with the necessary "pots and pans" to use until our moving van arrived. This was three weeks later!

It was such an adjustment for the family. One of us was still in Georgia. We were without a congregation of our own. We "belonged" to no one. We were in an entirely new culture of people, customs, food. Also, our work was entirely different and had to be "learned as we went along." And to top it off, we were all homesick and wanted to go home. I tried to encourage the family, as well as myself. After all, I told them, we were assigned for a four-year term, and we had never reneged on any commitment.

THE DAY A VISION CAME TRUE

As part of looking over our new home and work place, I went downstairs to the basement of the house. This was where the State Office was located. There was one room with a very low ceiling. In fact, it was so low I could hardly stand up. The room contained the furnace for the house, two desks, a filing cabinet, and three chairs. This made up the State Office. The overseer and the youth director would work together in this one room.

One of the most unexpected and unexplainable things ever to occur in my ministry happened when I stepped into that basement room that morning. Over twenty years before, when Rachel and I were still in Bible School, I had had a vision. Sister Barth had called a time of fasting and prayer to clear up a problem in the school. On the third day of fasting and prayer, we students were in a classroom, down on our knees praying. I was over against the wall, calling out to God.

Suddenly I was swept away from the classroom into a vision of the future. I saw what my work would be in serving God.

Rachel and I were traveling a long road that kept going up hill. We always were traveling toward the sun, with the wind in our face. The farther we traveled the more alone we were. Finally, we arrived at the destination, a place where we ministered to many nationalities—Indians, Blacks, and others. For years I remembered this vision and wondered about it. Finally, I decided that it must have just been symbolic, just a dream I had in Bible School.

But that day when I stepped into the State Office in the basement of that old house on North 10th Avenue in Yakima, Washington, I knew that this appointment was the fulfillment of that vision. Preaching and working for God in Washington state were what that vision had pointed to al-most two decades ago. We had traveled the long road going up hill, always looking toward the sun, with the wind in our face. It had just taken us twenty years to get to our destination!

I didn't know the specifics that morning, just how and where we'd be ministering to many nationalities. But I knew Washington state was where this would happen. I wasn't surprised, then, when within days we were preaching on two Indian reservations at the edge of town. Within weeks we were preaching to Oriental con-gregations and at the East Pasco Church of God to a fine congregation of Black worshipers. (It was at the East Pasco church that one wonderful church member raised her arms in praise to God, saying, "We had a good state overseer and we were sorry to see him go. But now we've got another good overseer. God had another ram caught in the bush!)

NOBODY HAS WHAT YOU WANT

Just a few weeks after we arrived in Yakima, the State Prayer Conference was scheduled to be held. Brother Wade Horton from General Headquarters would be coming out to be with us for this conference. He would be staying at our house. Rachel wanted to prepare a special meal.

I went down to the grocery store. Everything, of course, was unfamiliar to me, so I went up and down the aisles, looking for what I wanted. I couldn't find anything.

"Where is the self-rising flour?" I asked the store manager, whom I saw in the aisle.

"The what?" he answered.

"I'd like some self-rising flour and some self-rising corn meal," I told him.

"I've never heard of that," he replied. "What is it? And who makes it?"

I calmly explained to him the principle of salt, baking powder, and soda already being added to the flour and meal so that the bread would rise of its own accord while it bakes. I told him that big companies like Gold Medal and White Lily and lots of others made this mixture and sold it in all sizes of bags—two pounds, five pounds, ten pounds. He was amazed.

"Wow," he said, "If you had that you wouldn't have to use yeast and knead your bread so it would rise, would you? I think I'll order some for the store."

I told him I thought that would be a great idea. (In the four years we lived there, we never saw self-rising flour or meal on the shelf.)

Anxious to get the rest of the things on my list, I asked the manager, "Where are your sweet potatoes?"

"Sweet potatoes?" he asked. "Sweet potatoes. Oh, we don't have any sweet potatoes, but we do have some yams."

I was about as aggravated as a preacher can be. "For goodness sakes, then, give me some yams!" I got those yams and lit out for the house. I was ready to be home.

LEARNING HOW

The kind of work we did every day was completely new to us. I felt helpless and lost. There was nobody for me to go visit in the hospital; there were no members who needed me to come to their house to pray.

"What does an overseer do?" I asked Rachel the first day we went down to work in the office. "Where do we start?"

Rachel said, "We'll just have to learn the work as we go along."

And we did.

We worked hard to organize new churches and shore up established churches all over the state. On a lot of Sunday mornings we would drive two hundred miles or more to be in Sunday School at one of these churches. The children always complained because no matter how far we had traveled to get to the church, we were always the first ones there. They'd say, "Daddy, we could have slept another hour this morning! Why do we have to be at a church before the doors are opened?" We'd return to Yakima that night so the children could be back in school and Rachel and I could be back in the State Office on Monday morning.

The work we had to do included at times some unpleasant things. One of the churches in the state was in a dispute over clauses in the church deed. These clauses determined who owned the building. This pastor was threatening to go independent. He said the building belonged to him and he was going to continue to use it after he left the Church of God. I, of course, was representing the interests of the Church. I said he was not going to take the church building when he left. That building, I told him, belongs to the Church of God.

The situation got very ugly. I had never been involved in anything like this so it probably bothered me more than it would have someone who was used to handling legal affairs. I couldn't sleep at night. I thought about the situation every day, trying to figure out some way to work it out.

I did know one thing to do and that was to pray. So I sought the wisdom of God. "Show me, Lord," I prayed, "what I ought to do."

I also called General Headquarters and got advice and direction from them. It soon became clear what action we had to take.

I hired a lawyer to represent the Church of

God. The preacher hired a lawyer to represent him. The lawyers went back and forth. Rachel and I would get phone calls almost every day in the State Office about this matter. Instead of things working out, however, they seemed to get worse. It was a long, drawn-out thing.

One night I was away from home, preaching across the state at Tacoma. The phone rang at the house, and Rachel answered it. A voice threatened, "This law suit is a serious matter. There is no telling how it is going to wind up. Tell your husband that things are going to get messy before everything is over." Rachel, of course, was scared to death.

Finally, everything did work out. The case was settled out of court. The church remained the property of the Church of God. The pastor was given what the lawyers agreed was a fair amount to compensate him for his work on the church. The situation had been a real ordeal for a preacher and his wife who had no experience in this kind of thing. Rachel and I were glad it was over.

WE COME TO LOVE THE LIFE

The state had a campground of 160 acres on a mountain out of Woodland, Washington. This was a beautiful camp. The ministers of the state had built nice cabins on the campground. There was a caretaker who lived there all the time and looked after the camp. Here we had our camp meetings, youth camps, and council meetings.

We always loved to go over the mountain to spend a few days while working on that side of the state. It was a treat to visit Brother Barber, the caretaker. He would always have a big salmon, just caught, dressed and ready for cooking, when we would go over.

Brother Barber was one of the greatest men that I have ever known and a strong Christian. You were blessed to be with him and to hear his stories of living a logger's life. He had been a logger all his life and was now retired. His axes were so sharp a man could shave with them. And many loggers did. When the loggers had a tree-topping contest or a logrolling or a logcutting,

Brother Barber would take me. It was amazing to watch these men in these contests. They could climb a tree, cut the top out of it, and then get down so quickly. (I have today an ax Brother Barber gave me that he used in the woods.)

*   *   *

I loved to go to the Indian churches. They would give us wild game, elk, deer, and oysters when we visited there. One rainy day a great old Indian man took me salmon fishing on a small creek. The Indian was working a line with salmon that were going upstream to spawn. I was not allowed to fish because we were on an Indian reservation; but the Indian would catch the fish, dress them, and leave them on the bank for me to pick up. He said, "You can't fish, but what you find you can take home with you."

*   *   *

Needless to say, we became lovers of Washington state and enjoyed a wonderful four years there. The snow, mountain passes, tunnels, Cascade Mountains, and beautiful woods added to our way of life. All year long we could look across miles and miles and see snow-covered mountains from our parsonage. One July, the children had a "snowball throwing" contest at the foot of Mount Rainier.

Barbara had her surprise sweet sixteen birthday party in Yakima, and Frank received his first bicycle while we lived there. Elizabeth came home after she graduated from college and taught school in Yakima. For a year the family was together again.

I was gone much of the time, traveling around the state. Rachel and the family couldn't go with me during the week. This had its disadvantages, but they found out also that it had at least one advantage. I was never a "sandwich" man; I always wanted hot food and biscuits for a meal. But when I was gone, the family got to eat sandwiches to their heart's content. This they dearly loved.

I bought the girls an old Buick to use to travel back and forth to school. Rachel and the children also used the car to go to church while I was away. The old Buick had more acceleration than it had brakes, so I understand they had many exciting times riding in that old car.

We did not know where we would be assigned at the General Assembly in 1964, so we did what we could do. We stored our things with the moving company with instructions we would call them when we knew where we were moving. We were quite a laughing matter.

"We're moving," we would announce.

Somebody would ask, "Where are you going?"

We'd reply, "We don't know—but we're moving!"

At the close of the 1964 General Assembly in Dallas, Texas, our name was called out for state overseer of Arkansas. So the call went forth to the moving company in Yakima, Washington. "Send our load to Little Rock, Arkansas. #2 Wanda Lane."

The years in Washington state were fruitful. With youth director Bob Moore and his wife Donna, Tommie and Rachel brought the state to a self-supporting status in two years. Many new churches were organized. Also in the first two years they bought a new State Parsonage and built a new State Office. The State Office contained the state overseer's office, the youth director's office, a reception room, a council room, and a printing room. This was a long way from the one-room office in the furnace room of the basement on North 10th Avenue.

The move to Arkansas brought new opportunities. Arkansas had eighty Churches of God. This meant the duties of the overseer were more extensive. The years in Washington had provided training and experience, however, that empowered Tommie and Rachel in their new tasks.

Bob and Donna Moore moved to Arkansas with the Harpers and spent two profitable years building up the state. Then Ralph and Aurelia Brewer and their family joined the state team as youth director, completing the four-year term. Many new churches were organized; buildings were constructed; churches remodeled. At the end of the four-year appointment, all the state's debt had been paid and there was a surplus in the treasury.

One of the things Tommie Harper has done throughout his ministry is to emphasize old-fashioned preaching and singing. None of this modern way for him. He believes in sermons being preached the way they were in the olden days, and he loves the old-time songs. One year in Arkansas he was able to have a dream of his come true.

THE YEAR THE CAMP MEETING SONGS STOPPED TRAFFIC

T he third year we were in Arkansas, I asked the state council to buy new song books for camp meeting. "Let's get the old-fashioned hymnal and sing the songs that churches used to sing many years ago, songs people will be able to sing even without the book." The council agreed. So when camp meeting began that year, we had the old-fashioned Church of God hymnal for the choir.

The camp ground was on Route 64 up near Bald Knob, north of Little Rock. Elizabeth and Barbara came for camp meeting. Elizabeth played the piano, Barbara played the organ, and Frank sang in the choir.

The young people would gather an hour early before service each evening and start singing. The choir leader would say, "Turn to page ninety-four."

The group would start to sing: "The Lord has been so good to me, He set my captive spirit free; Old things are passed away, all things are new today; He gave me light for paths so dim, O how I've changed since I found him, I'm in a new world since the Lord saved me."

Every time I heard that song I remembered the night in Digby, Georgia, when I looked up through a ragged hole in that tent and saw stars that had never been there before. "I'm in a New World" was a song that spoke to me.

Then they'd sing the old spiritual, "Just a Little Talk with Jesus." I would feel like shouting when I heard words like: "I may have doubts and fears, my eyes be filled with tears, But Jesus is a Friend Who watches day and night; I go to Him in prayer, He knows my ev'ry care, And just a little talk with Jesus makes it right."

The entire congregation would join in when the young people began to sing "I'll Fly Away." You couldn't help but be uplifted by words like, "Some glad morning when this life is o'er, I'll fly away; To a home on God's celestial shore, I'll fly away. I'll fly away, O glory, I'll fly away; When I die, hallelujah, by and by, I'll fly away."

Someone in the audience would make a request: Sing "When the Roll is Called Up Yonder." You could hear the words loud and clear: "When the trumpet of the Lord shall sound, and time shall be no more, And the morning breaks eternal bright and fair; When the saved of earth shall gather over on the other shore, And the roll is called up yonder, I'll be there." Listening, you'd feel the truth of that song in your soul.

Almost every night the young people would conclude by singing "Amazing grace, how sweet the sound, that saved a wretch like me. I once was lost but now I'm found, was blind but now I see." The melody of that beautiful old song would echo all over the hillside, a sound you could never forget.

About the second night of camp meeting we noticed something unusual. Cars were lining up on both sides of Highway 64 as far as we could see. Travelers were stopping to listen to the singing.

Within a short while there was a serious traffic problem. Those who hadn't parked on the sides of the road were going so slow that traveling was about at a standstill. I said to one of the council members, "We are going to have to have some help."

In a few minutes one of the highway patrol officers directing traffic came up to where I was. "Preacher," he said, "We've radioed for some extra support. Everybody is wanting to listen to these songs."

Every night after that the cars would stop on Route 64, park, and listen to the singing. Every night the highway patrol would bring extra help to direct traffic. Near the end of the camp meeting, I saw the officer in charge near the entrance to the tabernacle. I said as I went in, "Oh, you're not down on the highway tonight. It's good to have you up here."

He looked at me and smiled. "We've worked out a rotation system so every officer will get to work this spot at least once before the meeting is over. We can hear the singing a lot better up here."

That was a wonderful camp meeting.

* * *

The state work we did the four years in Arkansas and the four years in Washington gave us a wider range in our work. Things happened that led us to a deeper life in the Lord. Many times we found ourselves without an answer, maybe for both a church and a pastor. But always through fasting and prayer, we got an answer.

There are two songs that gave us strength in times of troubled waters: "The Answer is on the Way," and "He's Already Done What He Said He Would Do." We practiced trusting this in our work, and these words still play a great part in our lives today.

Church policy determined that an in-*dividual could serve no more than eight consecutive years as a state overseer. So in 1968 it was time for Tommie and Rachel to return to pastoring. Their appointment was to the Avondale Estates Church of God in Atlanta, a large urban church of several hundred members. They pastored the Avondale church for six satisfying years.*

The almost forty years Rachel and Tommie had spent in the Church of God had seasoned them. By now there had been so many times of calling on God—always to discover that He heard and answered the prayer—that Tommie had the kind of relationship with his heavenly Father that most people have with their telephone. He knew God was on the other end of the line. In every situation he trusted because he knew God was with him and beside him every minute of the day. This trust and faith worked even in the most difficult of times.

GOD, HELP ME FLY THIS PLANE

I t was early spring. Several of the men in the church suggested we all go on a fishing trip up to Santee Cooper Lake in South Carolina. We would fish for stripe, big fish. We decided to leave Atlanta in the afternoon so that we could get up to the fishing camp, where we had reservations, and be ready to hit the lake early the next morning. Several of the men drove in cars, and four of us flew in Lee Lindsey's four-seater Cessna. Lee was the choir director at the Avondale Church of God, a young man in his early forties, married to Mary Lindsey who played the piano at the church. They had two children.

We landed once during the two-hour flight. We had to refuel the plane, so we touched down in Orangeburg, South Carolina. After that stop, we headed straight for the landing strip at Santee Cooper Lake. On our way we flew over the little town of Santee, about forty-five minutes before we reached Santee Cooper, and made radio contact with the small airport there.

As we got near the Santee Cooper landing strip, we hit a storm. The weather was very bad, and we lost radio contact with the ground. We could not see the ground because there was so much fog and bad weather. Lee decided to fly out over the ocean about twenty miles to wait for the storm to clear up. He then turned the plane back toward land, but we still could not see the ground nor could we get radio contact.

For a second time, Lee took the plane back out over the ocean for about twenty miles, turned around, and came back to land at Santee Cooper. The fog was no better.

Lee said, "Let's go back out one more time; and then if we come back and can't land, we'll go to another airport."

Brother Green, one of the men in the back

seat of the plane, said, "Lee, why don't we go on to the Santee airport now. Let's not fly back out over the ocean again."

Lee said, "Oh, I think it's going to be clear by the time we get back," and he headed the plane out toward the waves.

I intervened and said, "Lee, maybe we should go on back to Santee. We can have someone from the fishing camp at Santee Cooper drive down and pick us up at Santee." Reluctantly, Lee agreed and turned the plane toward Santee.

We soon flew out of the storm. Lee said to me, "Preacher, you've never flown a plane before, have you? Want to take this one over?"

But Brother Hays in the back seat spoke up quickly: "Lee, you keep your hands on that equipment."

I said, "Yes, Lee, you better keep flying this thing, else these men in the back will get out and walk."

When we arrived at Santee, the sun was bright. The runway was in clear sight. Lee got clearance to land, but we had to circle for several minutes. Two little planes were sporting around on the runway, going up, circling around, dipping back down, touching the runway and then going back up. While we circled, Lee began to sing in his beautiful tenor voice, "Jesus is the Sweetest Name I Know."

Finally, there was an opening. The second plane had gone up, so Lee went in under him. He set all the instruments to land, and we started down for the runway.

Suddenly, without warning, Lee Lindsey fell over on my shoulder. I jerked around and lifted up his head.

"He's dead," I shouted to the men in the back.

"Can you land this thing?" the men asked frantically.

"I don't know," I replied, "but I'm sure going to try."

First, I prayed. "God, help me land this plane. Let me land this plane." Then, knowing that God was right there with me, I started to think: What did Lee do when we landed at Orangeburg? I did everything that I could possibly remember that he had done when the plane touched down. I pushed the throttle. I kept my hands tight on the wheel. I got ready to pull on the brake. We were going down.

When the plane hit the runway, I pulled the brake as hard as I could and I never let it go. We were going very fast when we touched down, so we bounced several times and skidded as I tried to brake us to a stop. Lee's head was still on my shoulder.

Finally, about twenty yards from the fence that enclosed the airstrip, the plane came to a stop. People standing around the airstrip had observed us landing the way we did. They knew something was wrong. So within seconds people had crowded all around the plane. One of the airport operators opened the door of the plane; he and I lifted Lee out. We stretched his body out on the wing.

"He's dead," the man said. There was a long pause. "And you three are lucky that you're not."

We knew we were.

Only minutes before, we had been flying twenty miles out over the ocean. Only seconds before Lee had his fatal heart attack, the instruments had been set. And when we needed Him the most, God had joined me in the pilot's seat. Together, He and I had landed that plane!

The family in 1954.
Tommie, Rachel, Elizabeth, Frank, and Barbara.

Mama.   *Papa.*

After the hunt.
Tommie with Snowball (standing)
and Old Tim (lying down).

Quail and gravy for supper tonight.

A good day's work for Snowball
and Queen.

Pleased with the hunt.
Tommie, son Frank (l), friend and
dogs Betty and Ruth.

PART IV

THE HARVEST
1974–1986

And he shall be like a tree planted by the rivers of water, that bringeth forth his fruit in his season; his leaf also shall not wither; and whatsoever he doeth shall prosper.

Psalms 1:3

Tommie was now sixty-six years old.
The six years he and Rachel pastored at Avondale Estates had been active ones. The church and parsonage had been remodeled and redecorated. The mortgage had been paid off; the church was now free of debt.

It was now time to return full circle. Tommie wanted to preach revivals. He and Rachel were going out in full-time evangelistic work.

WE MOVE TO POSSUM CREEK

After six good years with the Avondale Church of God, I felt the evangelistic fire burning in my soul. I decided to resign from pastoral work and preach revivals. We had no debts to worry about, and we had a five-room house on a big lake in Tennessee. So Rachel and I made our plans and worked toward them.

In the fall of 1974 I went to talk to the state overseer of Georgia, Brother Ray H. Hughes. He was puzzled. Why would a man pastoring a church that had no debt, where he had gotten eighty-nine percent of the vote for another four-year term, and where there was growth in every department, want to leave?

After we talked for a while and Brother Hughes still couldn't understand my decision, he looked at me and said, "Now, Brother Harper, please tell me why you want to leave pastoring to evangelize."

I answered him, "Brother Hughes, I am tired. And I feel we can do a great work for God on the field."

Brother Hughes then gave me his blessing.

He also said, "It takes a man that loves the Lord to give up a pay check every week to enter a field of work with no promise of a salary." Everything was quiet for a minute.

Then he said, "But, Brother Harper, if any man can do it, you can."

Those words were a staff that I leaned on in some of the bleak, lonely times that were ahead.

* * *

In November of 1974 we moved to our new home on Possum Creek.

We had a little five-room fishing cabin that we fixed up to be a year-round home. We built a 16x15 foot den with a big four-foot fireplace which we used the first two winters there. Then we put in a large Ashley wood heater which heats the house all through the bedrooms.

After we got settled in, we began working with the churches in the area. We had a good revival with the East Soddy Church of God and the Sale Creek Church of God. Then in the spring of 1975 we began to preach revivals in many states across the nation—Oklahoma, Arkansas, Oregon, Washington. We would be out for one to two months at a time.

We would try to plan these meetings to stay in one state for a month before going to another. Sometimes we preached twenty-nine times in one month. This would include three churches, leaving one church on Sunday night, starting with another on Monday night. Then we would travel whatever the distance to begin the next revival.

Some of the meetings would be with pastors that we did not know. Our first thoughts would be, "How did the church come to call us for this meeting?" The puzzle would be solved when we learned that we had been recommended by some other pastor that knew us and knew the kind of preaching I did.

Many times on the opening night of the revival, I would say, "Look us over tonight. We are new to you. You are strangers to us. But we have one thing in common, and that is the old-time gospel. I have no rabbits to pull out of the hat, nothing up my sleeve but my arm, no compromising of the gospel. But we'll fight the devil on all sides and declare that God will save."

*   *   *

One revival I preached in a little church in Oklahoma in 1975 stands out in my memory. We had received a letter from a friend asking if we would come to that church for a revival. The pastor also called and requested that we come. When we arrived, we found that we were to stay in the home of our friend who had been our member when we pastored the Rossville church.

The revival started and the Holy Ghost blessed the services. I often would have to wait to preach while the church rejoiced in the Spirit.

There was some old family trouble in the church, but I knew nothing about it. Night after night, however, God would lay it on my heart to preach on the same subject: the bed was too narrow and the cover too short.

I used as my Scripture Isaiah chapter twenty-eight, verses, nineteen and twenty: *"From the time that it goeth forth it shall take you: for morning by morning shall it pass over, by day and by night: and it shall be a vexation only to understand the report. For the bed is shorter than that a man can stretch himself on it: and the covering narrower than that he can wrap himself in it."*

I never start studying for a sermon until first I have sought the Lord about what He would have me tell the people. Sometimes I may carry in my mind a thought, but I first want to find God's will for the message. So I knew this was what God wanted me to preach.

The people in the church could see that my messages were not planned but were given by the direction of the Holy Ghost. Things started coming to light that had been covered for many years. Church members repented; families were reconciled. God blessed in a mighty way.

Rachel and I still hear from this little church and can see the fruit of our labor, which was not in vain. Some of the members taped the services each night, and they are still playing those tapes.

Tommie always preaches from an out-
line, *one he has written himself on a piece of white
paper—small enough to fit in his Bible—usually alter-
nating between a black and red pen. The black pen is for
the main points and the red for the Bible verses and the
supporting points.*

*Two of his earliest outlines can be found in the
Bible given to him on January 30, 1939, by Brother
George Allen, one of his teachers at Bible School. It was
this Bible which Tommie used when he preached in Bible
School and in those early revivals in south Georgia.*

*The two outlines are written on the back of a
small yellowed piece of paper. This paper on one side has
printed instructions entitled "Directions For Your Tent."
On the other side appear Tommie's two sermon outlines
and the beginning of a third. (Tommie had also copied
nine of the ten commandments on this side of the paper.)*

The printed side of the paper reads:

DIRECTIONS FOR YOUR TENT

– = –

This Tent is made with ropes in pockets, this Insures that the Strain is on the Ropes.

See that Ropes that run from Edge of Tent to the Peak of the Tent are guaged Just Right at All times, by taking up a little or letting out a little, as the case may be, keeping All Strain Off Canvas.

It is a true saying that the Wall of the Tent should come Up with the Sun so that the Dew will not dry out of the Tent with the Wall Down, thus causing your Tent to mildew or Rot. So don't Fail to give your Tent air in Three Ways Every Day.

1. Don't Ever take your Tent down when Wet or even Damp.

2. Don't allow Any One to walk on your Tent while laying flat on the ground.

3. Always Wrap Burlap around Bail Ring when rolling up your Tent.

4. If your Tent wants to Sag, draw up a little on your Tackle or Main Pole.

5. If there seems to be too many Border Poles, or Tent won't stretch out right, let your Tent down until it stretches out Right.

REV. L. P. SHAW

MANUFACTURER OF GOSPEL TENTS

VALDOSTA   GEORGIA

These were the instructions for the tent that Tommie used when he preached his first revival in the Church of God, at Broxton, Georgia, in the spring of 1941.

* * *

One of Tommie's sermon outlines written on the back of the "Directions for your Tent" reads:

Caring for the Church

Acts 20:28–38

Text. 20:35

Truths. 20:28–32
    I. Cor. 16:1–2

Example Acts 6:1–6
The choosing of the 7 deacons.

God wants a willing people. Acts 4:31–37

The danger of an untried life to the church. Acts 5:1–11.

The second outline reads:

What Scar Can Show For Jesus

Text. John 20:27

Unbelievers want to see the scar. John 20:25

What will God accept. Micah 6:6–7

What God requires of man.
Micah 6:8

The third outline—only a title and a text—reads:

What Do You See In Others?

Luke 6:39–44

Text. 2 Sam. 12:7

As the years went on, Tommie's sermon outlines were more detailed than these three from his earliest days of preaching. They had names like "The Touch of Jesus"; "What Does Man Get Out Of Life?"; "Working For A Bonus"; "How Are You Building?"; "A Man Sent From God"; "God Working in the Time of Crisis"; "What Seek Ye?"; "Our High Priest"; "The Traveler's Map"; "What Are These Among So Many?" "I Would That You Knew My God"; "The Family's Place in the Church and the Home"; "My God Is Real, Is Yours?"; "Unity"; "The Church and Its Benefits"; "What is Man?"; "God Calls Your Number"; "Called But No Answer."

Tommie keeps all of his outlines, often preaching a sermon many times in different parts of the country. On the back of each outline he notes when and where the sermon was preached. "What Does Man Get Out of Life?" he preached first on January 5, 1949, and again on January 6, 1984, as well as seven other times in between.

The outline for that sermon reads:

What Does Man Get Out Of Life?

Ecclesiastes 1:3

What profit hath a man of all his labour which he taketh under the sun?

I. Solomon talks as one that knows. He was born with a silver spoon in his mouth. He tried everything but found nothing to stand: 40,000 horses; 12,000 horsemen; 700 wives; 300 concubines; 30 measures of fine flour, and threescore measures of meal; an annual income of 666 talents of gold. He wrote 3000 proverbs and 1005 songs.

II. Everyone of us wants to be satisfied, but the world can't give satisfaction. Many men and women who will have 1949 carved on their tombstones will have tried to get satisfaction in this life but failed.

III. Stories of men who did not find the most in this life but in the hereafter: Noah, Moses, Abraham, Stephen. (II Kings 5:3; Judges 6:15.)

IV. This world is not meant to be our home. John takes the old pen and writes in I John 3:1, "Behold, what manner of love the Father hath bestowed upon us, that we should be called the sons of God: therefore, the world knoweth us not, because it knew him not."

(Luke 16:22; II Timothy 4:7−8)

The sermon "I Would That You Knew My God" was preached nine times from 1960 to 1982. This is the outline for that sermon:

I Would That You Knew My God

II Kings 5:3; Hebrews 11:1

There is help for man in every walk of life. Our standings or position have no bearing on God. (Choosing of the disciple Matthew and talking to Zaccheus.)

The man of God has and will fail. But the God of man will never fail. To know God will give joy even in the face of opposition. (II Samuel 6:13–14; the god of the Golden Calf, Exodus 32:4; god of Baal, I Kings 18:27; John 5:5–7; John 9:1–7.)

To know God will give us strength when all help has seemed to fail. (I Kings 18:36; I Samuel 17:45; II Kings 6:16–17)

There is no other place or god to go to. John 6:66–68.
The God that never faileth (Acts 3:16)

The beginning and the end.

Our God is above all other gods that man can worship, even above all forces of man. Daniel 3:16–18; 24–25; John 3:1–2

Acts 9:4–6 (Paul's life) Acts 24:14

When Jesus died the sun quit shining; mountains crumbled before the place.

John 4:29 "Come, see a man, which told me all things ever that I did: Is not this the Christ?"

"The Touch of Jesus" is another sermon preached from the 1940s through the 1980s. Here is that outline:

The Touch of Jesus

Matt. 8:3.

And Jesus put forth his hand, and touched him, saying, I will; be thou clean. And immediately his leprosy was cleansed.

The touch of Jesus makes the difference in the world.

His touch blesses the children.
Mark 10:13–16

His touch heals.
Luke 22:51; Matt. 9:29–30; Matt. 8:15; Matt. 17:7

There was the touch of Jesus that changed the calendar. Before Christ. The Year of Our Lord.

Palestine itself, although of great meaning to the Jews, never became The Holy Land until Jesus had touched it.

David looked at the star-studded heavens and wondered how and why God should give any attention to man.

These outlines came to life in the pulpit. Many of the revivals Tommie Harper preached were interdenominational city-wide or area-wide meetings. After one such revival, the pastor of the local First Baptist Church described what it was like when Tommie preached:

> We will see the fruits of this city-wide camp meeting for years to come. If you come to hear Tommie Harper preach looking for a class of dress, you won't find it here. This man's pulpit manners could be called crude and without grace. He's not into his message very far before off comes his glasses. Then his coat is next. With his coat he wipes his face, slings it over his head, wipes his face again, and throws the coat on the chair. When he picks it up again, it is to use it as a handkerchief. All the time his message of love and power is coming with thunder and lightening. As he preaches, conviction can be felt.

*   *   *

In the years of preaching revivals after moving to Possum Creek, Tommie always did his best to be home during the spring and summer. It was time to put in the garden. During these months Tommie would hold revivals close around home, preach on Sundays, Wednesday and Friday nights at local churches, and serve as interim pastor when someone like Reverend Lewis Hickman, pastor of the East Soddy Church of God, went on vacation.

During each day he would work in his garden— which might more accurately be referred to as a mini-farm. On the plot, which was almost an acre, Tommie cultivated peanuts, pumpkins, watermelons, corn, green peppers, cucumbers, tomatoes, okra, beans, peas, cabbage, cantaloupes, onions, squash, turnips, butterbeans, collards, and sweet potatoes. His tools were a cultivator and a tiller which he pushed and a hoe.

HOW DOES YOUR GARDEN GROW?

I tried to plan our meetings so we could be in driving distance of home from April through August or September. This meant I could grow a big garden to have fresh vegetables through the summer and fill our two freezers and can two or three hundred jars of food for the winter. It was a beautiful sight to go into our kitchen and see the long shelves on each side of the walls filled with canned food. Then behind the door there were shelves built six or seven feet high which were also filled. (I believe you can still live off of the land.)

We canned for the children as well as ourselves and gave them fresh corn, beans, tomatoes, okra, and many other things. They thought there was nothing like what came from Daddy's home-grown garden. Rachel made her famous fourteen-day pickles. They are known as the best from Georgia to Texas. The children would come in and tell Rachel, "We're out of pickles." They would never go home without them, because Rachel would not forget.

One Father's Day our daughter Barbara and her husband Will gave me a day's work in the garden as a Father's Day present. This work day came after a rainy spell. The grass was thick; the weather, hot. Their job was to hoe out the watermelons. This they did. But they have been very careful in giving work days for presents ever since.

I also started growing corn right after we moved to Possum Creek, the kind of corn you use to make corn meal. After the corn got dry, I would shell it, using an old-fashioned corn sheller. Then Rachel and I would carry it over to an old grist mill about seventeen miles from home and get it ground. We would have home-ground meal for the year, for us and the children.

Give me a glass of buttermilk with a pone of corn bread, and I'm in second heaven and ready to fight the giants of life to prove to the city dudes what living is. There is so much that country living offers that will never be known by this world. It is a pity it is being lost to this generation and will never be redeemed again.

Tommie and Rachel soon became a

part of the community at Possum Creek. Their small house is located on the premises of an old fishing club, established in 1940, known as the Chickamauga Fly and Bait Casting Club. The Chickamauga Fly and Bait Casting Club is located in the Soddy-Daisy, Tennessee, community, thirty-five miles north of Chattanooga. Approximately thirteen families live on the grounds of the club. The club is governed by individuals elected from the membership. The members meet monthly to conduct the business of the club and to socialize with each other. Several other retired couples, in addition to Tommie and Rachel, live at Chickamauga Fly and Bait Casting Club. (Tommie is quick to tell you, however, that he is retired from pastoring but not from preaching.)

Not long after Tommie and Rachel had settled in at Possum Creek, the editor of the club newsletter wrote this:

Here at Possum Creek he is called Mr. Harper, Reverend Harper, Preacher Harper, just plain Preacher and Tommie.

In addition to being a husband and a father, he is the gardener. In between gardening hours, he has time to be a fisherman. You can see him taking off in his boat from real early in the morning until late in the afternoon or early evening. Usually, he has his big bucket with his minnow bucket inside it and five or six fishing rods. And he uses them all. If he doesn't get out in the boat, he can be found at the end of the boat dock with his rods all baited and waiting for a bite. He keeps Rachel stocked with fish for her Weight Watcher's Program.

Tommie is a carpenter. I overheard him recently asking about some 2x4's to build a chicken coop. He must be the one who has that darn ole rooster that crows every morning and lets the neighbors know it is time to get up.

Tommie is Building and Grounds Chairman of the Chickamauga Fly and Bait Casting Club, which is not an easy job. You must see the retaining walls that are patched with concrete, the fishing pier ramp that has been rebuilt and listen to the usual complaints to appreciate the job he has done. These are things he has been involved in this year.

About Rachel, the newsletter editor wrote:

Rachel Harper? Who is she? What does she do?

She is a wife and has been married close to fifty years to Tommie Harper. She is a mother with three children who with their spouses make six.

She is a cook; three meals a day are prepared in her kitchen. She is a laundry woman, and on pretty days can be seen hanging out her clothes in the sun to dry.

She is a food processor. Not only does Rachel can the vegetables from their garden, but she makes the best fourteen-day pickles, to which the members of the Chickamauga Fly and Bait Casting Club will attest. She dries apples in early summer, makes jelly, and in the fall after the first frost she grinds and mixes up the best sausage you've ever tasted.

She is a seamstress. She has made clothing for herself and has altered many of her dresses. It was a necessity. A year ago she joined Weight Watchers and lost thirty-four pounds. She is an inspiration to those who go every Tuesday night; she has nothing but words of encouragement for the other Weight Watchers who are not as strong-willed and self-disciplined as she is. She reached her goal and maintains her weight.

Rachel is an artist. She is creative with her hands. She crochets and does many kinds of handwork. She is a member of the Possum Creek Handcraft Society—ladies who live on the club grounds and meet every Wednesday to exchange ideas, talk, bring a sandwich, and enjoy the fellowship of each other.

Rachel is a traveler. When she travels, it's for weeks at a time. To Georgia, Arkansas, Washington state, Texas. For revivals or to visit family and friends.

Last of all, Rachel Harper is a sweet, kind, thoughtful person who is devoted to her church and her Lord Jesus.

We are happy to have this Georgia Belle and Georgia Cracker as our friends and neighbors.

Not long after Tommie and Rachel *moved to Possum Creek, Tommie had something happen while he was fishing that could have ruined his reputation from the very start.*

CHASING THE BAIT

If you are to be a good fisherman, you must prepare. As spring opens up, you hope to go fishing every day; and you soon learn the good spots to fish. After I discovered the good places to fish in the spring at Possum Creek, I would bait these areas with dog food, corn, and chicken mash.

With the dog food, I would punch holes in the top and bottom of the can. This would let the food seep out as the fish turned the cans on the bottom of the lake. The corn I used as I fished, throwing a handful around where I was fishing. This would cause the fish to take the bait. The chicken mash I put in a paper sack with holes cut into the top and a rock put in the bottom to help the sack sink. This baiting I would do a day or two before I started fishing.

One day while talking with some other fishermen, I found out that you could use panty hose to put the bait in instead of a can or paper sack. My first try at doing this was a tragedy.

I was out on the lake on a windy day. I had filled some of Rachel's old panty hose with a can of dog food in each toe. Then at the knees I had put another can of dog food. This I thought was heavy enough to cause the panty hose to sink to the bottom.

But when I threw them out into the water, they did not sink at all. The panty hose, looking just like a pair of woman's legs, started floating away, the current and wind carrying them down the lake.

By the time I could get my motor started, those legs were a long way away. I raced the boat as fast as I could toward the legs. When I had almost reached them, the wind whipped them off in another direction. I raced with the boat over there. This went on for several minutes. It was like chasing your hat when it has been blown off your head by a strong wind.

There I was, the new preacher in the community, chasing these legs all over the lake. I kept looking up to the boat dock to see if anyone was watching me. I wanted to retrieve those panty hose before someone reported me for a murder or a drowning. So I learned the hard way to use something heavy to sink those panty hose to the bottom. I still use this kind of bait, but I make sure the bait is going to sink!

In 1978 the three Harper children

honored their parents with a reception. It was Tommie and Rachel's fortieth year in the ministry. This was a festive occasion. White daisies were on every table. There was a cake with a church on top. Barbara needle-pointed a wall hanging depicting each place Tommie and Rachel had lived while serving in the Church of God: Bridgeford, Hazlehurst, Rossville, Yakima, Avondale, and Possum Creek. The children prepared four scrapbooks which contained photographs, clippings, drawings, and letters commemorating their parent's ministry for the past four decades. Many, many friends came to the reception to greet Tommie and Rachel on this special day.

Others who could not attend—church leaders and officials, old friends, members of the family—took the reception as an occasion to write letters communicating to Tommie and Rachel their love, their appreciation, and their memories.

Reverend A. V. Beaube, Tommie's first state overseer, sent this letter:

April 1, 1978

Rev. Tommie Harper:

Soon after you and I first met one could see that you were called and anointed, very sincere, and at the tender age of 33 you were an excellent preacher. Your lovely wife complimented your ministry with her dedicated life and ability.

The Georgia State Office furnished you a small ragged tent with no equipment to begin your ministry with the Church of God in Broxton, Ga. Although your educational and experimental ability was above the average beginner, you accepted it humbly, went to the woods and cut some poles, got together some seats, and began the revival which culminated with the organization of a Church of God.

I was proud of you and very happy to sign your first application to the ministry with the church May 13, 1941. Your faithfulness and ability was soon recognized and you were ordained and appointed as District Overseer of the Hazlehurst District.

. . . I have kept an ear to the ground for you over these years and have always been proud of you and Sister Harper.

I wish for you a long and happy life in your retirement and an abundant entrance into the everlasting kingdom of God.

Rev. A. V. Beaube

The General Overseer of the Church of God in 1978, Reverend Cecil Knight, wrote this to Tommie and Rachel:

Your dedication and commitment to Christ and to the church has marked your entire ministry. Brother Harper, you have been known as a churchman, as a man of convictions, and a man that is consistent in both life and ministry.

I remember the times that we had fellowship together. Especially my visit with you in the state of Washington while you served as overseer. You have left your mark of leadership and devotion wherever you have served and we are grateful to you for it.

Reverend Ray H. Hughes, an Assistant General Overseer in 1978, sent a letter, excerpted here:

During these four decades of dedicated service you have made a tremendous impact upon the people whom you have served. Your ministry has been broad and varied, taking you from the Deep South to the extreme Northwest, back to the Midwest, and now to Tennessee.

Wherever you have gone your ministry has been a savor of life and the people have respected you because you have practiced what you preached. You have lived the poetry that you have sung and you have made the principles of your faith the practice of your living. . . .

Reverend Robert Herrin, pastor of the Doraville Church of God in Atlanta and a recognized leader in the Church of God in the state of Georgia, wrote this letter. Tommie Harper helped Robert get started in the ministry.

I am writing you in my own hand because of the very personal nature of this letter.

First, let me say I deeply love you both. You stepped into my life at a critical time. As a young minister I needed the strength and warmth of a mature man of God. You were just that. Your love and acceptance of me was genuine and I thank you.

Thank you for "a home away from home." Thank you for sharing your wonderful family with me. Liz, Barbara, and Frank are "special" people to me not only because of their individuality but because they are part of you. I am sure your godly sincere lives have made an indelible spiritual impression upon their lives.

Thank you for your contribution to the Church of God. Many young men rise up and call you blessed because of your willingness to assist them. . . . The churches you have pastored love you deeply. The states you served are enriched, and everyone you have won to Christ are eternally grateful. May God richly bless you on this very special occasion. I love you and wish I could be with you. . . .

One of your boys,
Robert

WHAT IT WAS LIKE TO BE A PREACHER'S KID

In 1978 our children gave Rachel and me a reception to honor us in our fortieth year in the ministry. As part of this occasion, each child wrote a letter to Rachel and me. They talked about what it had been like growing up as a preacher's kid.

When Barbara was little, she always used to get so mad when people would say, "The preacher always has the meanest kids." She was feisty anyway, but that would really get her going.

She'd pipe back, "Well, that's just because they have to play with the members' children!"

Rachel and I used to worry about things the children were having to do without. In many ways they did not get to lead a normal life. They went to church in their first eighteen years probably more than most people go in an entire lifetime. We'd take them everywhere we went, and we usually went somewhere to church four or five nights a week. They had to learn to do their homework in the car. The girls had to learn how to roll their hair in the car on the way back home. There were many things all three of the children didn't get to do in school because they had to set a good example. This was often very hard.

But God blessed them and they seemed to grow up without any scars. Each one has grown up to be a mature, responsible adult. They all graduated from college with an advanced degree—Elizabeth, a Ph.D., Barbara, a Master's plus, and Frank, a law degree. Each of them has worked hard and made a mark in the world.

I had often wondered what the children thought as adults about being brought up as a preacher's kid. The letters they wrote to Rachel and me for the reception in 1978 answered my question.

Elizabeth

Dear Mother and Daddy:

Your forty years in the ministry and what they have meant to me:

One of my earliest memories is being on the platform at the Hazlehurst Church in a little yellow flowered dress wanting to sing a song. It must have been Sunday night, and I wasn't going to get to sing. I was crying. Then Daddy announced that I was going to sing. I jumped up and ran to the front of the stage. Daddy said, "Now, she's laughing and crying at the same time." And I began to sing with great happiness, "Climb, Climb Up Sunshine Mountain."

From the earliest times, the church was the pivot of my life. I liked being the preacher's daughter, even if it did mean being an example. (Daddy used to say, "You may not be a Christian, but you're going to act like one!) It let me stand out in the crowd. At camp meeting and youth camp, I was always pleased to be Tommie Harper's daughter, because he was an important man.

I remember Mother used to "preach" when Daddy was away. She would be in charge on prayer meeting night, and she always got up a wonderful little "sermon." She would do things like spell out a word—such as *prayer* or *behold*—and have Bible verses and information about each letter that taught the Spiritual truth she intended to make clear. I always loved to get up youth programs and Sunday School lessons, and I would often do the way she did in her talks. Today I still find that I use many of Mother's techniques when I prepare seminars.

One thing that your ministry means to me that I could not do without: my love to eat!

I remember with pleasure the company meals we would have when a visiting preacher was at the church. Mother would have a little menu taped inside the kitchen cabinet (something she still does), but somehow we almost always forgot the frozen lima beans. I would have to dust specially when we had company for supper all the rungs of the dining room chairs. Mother would ask me specifically if I had done that.

And I loved to eat after church! Especially on Sunday nights. We might have cheese hash or beef hash or black walnut ice cream (if I could get Barbara to ask Daddy to get some when we took Sister Hicks home!) or left-over cold dressing. If there was company, Daddy would tell stories from his boyhood which I loved to hear and if there wasn't company just the four or five of us would sit there having our after-church snack. . . .

I always loved to hear Mother sing in the choir. Even now, when I go to church with you, I'll have my book open, singing along, but I am really listening to Mother.

My pride knows no bounds when it comes to my family. How can I tell what you mean to me? I can't.

"Please tell me why
The sun does shine.
Please tell me why
The ivy twines.
Please tell me why
The sky's so blue.
Then I will tell you why
I love you."

You're as deep to me as the sky and the sun
and the grass and the trees. You are integrity
and realness and honesty and truth. I've never
needed to learn it anywhere else. You've stood
by me. (Daddy said, "She's my daughter.")
You've guided me; you've inspired me. The
older I've gotten the more I have loved you.

I love you sitting by the fire, your fishing,
your magazine pile, your home-made sausage,
your messy telephone book, your Bibles, your
woodpile, your flower beds, your garden, your
canned tomatoes, your chili, soup and stew,
your strawberry rolls, your rocking chairs, your
pick up truck, the poems you write, your sermon outlines, your crocheted place mats, your
strong bodies, your letters and drawings, your
interest in our work and our friends, your tea-
cakes, your Sunday School books, your church
Reporters, your fishing boat, your peach trees
that the squirrels always get, your pickles, your
fruitcake, your special table cloths for when
the kids come home, your offering to loan me
some money out of your savings when you
thought I might need it, the way people love
you, the way you always have to be at church
(or anywhere else) early, the devotional books

you read at breakfast, your giving parties for the children in Barbara's classes, your love for the Mission Field, your total and complete contribution to the work of God for forty years, and finally . . .

I thank you for your contribution to me. I will always be *your* daughter.

Love,

Sister

Barbara

As I think back over my childhood and life with my family, I'm filled with many happy memories. Although I can't begin to list them all, I'd like to share some of them with you.

Even though church and church activities were the hub of our life, you never once neglected our needs as children growing up in an everyday world. I want to share some of the "little" things that I remember from way back—which, in turn, proves that they were "big" things all along!

We were living on West Gordon Avenue, right across from the church. Daddy had gone visiting to invite people to church. When he got home, he said to me, "Go and look out in the garage." There was the most beautiful red scooter you have ever seen! Boy, did I feel important scooting around with Daddy holding me up to get me started.

Next came the new parsonage on Andrews
Street. That full-sized basement was so fas-
cinating to me. I can still recall hearing Daddy
down there praying. And no wonder you two
have been so successful. Mother was always
praying upstairs, too! I loved having "Vacation Bible School" in the big basement. Daddy
would save Sunday School literature for me,
and I'd round up the neighborhood kids. Vacation Bible School would last two weeks, and
we'd always end up with a little party that
Mother helped me with. Another thing I remember was that I'd go out on the front porch
and sing and try to preach like Daddy, who
would come home from visiting and tell me
to quiet down—that he heard me two blocks
away.

Another fond memory was going on pastoral
visits with Daddy. I'd sit in the lobby for hours
at Erlanger Hospital, just to get to ride back
and forth with Daddy.

You know, I can still remember some of
my new dresses that Mother made for me. It
seemed every time we had a district fellowship meeting or some "special" service, Mother
would get busy and make Sister and me a new
dress. I felt so special, and to this day I think a
new outfit is required for something special. At
Christmas one year Mother made Sister and
me satin dresses, one red and one green. And
you still do special things for us and make us
feel important.

As the years went on and we moved to
Washington State, we shared even more. It
was hard adjusting to being a State Overseer

rather than a pastor, but you two did adjust and well. I remember how everyone would comment on your just being one of them. They seemed to be surprised that you didn't act "high and mighty." They had just never known you. You two are always the same, no matter which position you are in or where you are. I appreciate that trait in you.

Then you went to Little Rock, and I went off to Lee College. I'll always remember that sick feeling of being "left" when you returned home. Frank and I had been together so long; I just didn't think I could manage without my "little brother." Having Sister close by in Chattanooga did help, though.

I feel that the consistency of your Christian living and sincere love of others made a deep impression in my life. The good, solid foundation in our family has meant a lot to me. It is a real pleasure to help in this celebration of your forty years in the ministry. I'm glad God gave you to me as parents. If I could go back in time, I would choose the very same parents and brother and sister. I get such a good feeling when Will and I start up that road to HOME.

I would also choose our lives revolving around church and home. I feel that values and attitudes were taught to me that have molded my entire life. May God bless you as you have blessed our family and others.

I love you,

Barbara

Frank

One of the brightest recollections I have of growing up as the son of a minister is that my father's profession was always good for a comment. When you're a kid, one of the first things you find out about a new classmate or a new friend is what their father does, and I cannot count the times when someone from the church would introduce me as "our preacher's son . . ." and, invariably, someone would have a comment about preachers' kids being the meanest or about how I sure did not act like a preacher's kid or some such poppycock! I must confess, though. I never really minded the comments or the jokes; they provided me with a little notoriety because there never were many preacher's kids in the crowd.

On a more serious note, I honestly believe that my father being a pastor and overseer provided our family with invaluable experiences. We got to live in several sections of the country, thus experiencing different customs, climates, and an infinite variety of other things. Also, as the pastor's or overseer's family, we often entertained in our home. I believe these experiences helped us all in our ability to deal with people and to be before the public.

I am sure you often wonder how two such calm and stable people like you could have produced three kids who are apt to pop up anywhere at any time. Believe it or not, you get credit for this, too, and, yes, I mean credit

because this is a positive part of our person-
alities. I remember when we moved to Washington. We did not know a soul out there, and
instead of just moving into a new neighborhood across town we moved across the country. Compared to this, my going away to school
in Wisconsin or Elizabeth's going to work in
New York or Barbara and Will cutting loose in
Charlotte and moving back to Cleveland are
really not that hard to understand. Being with
you and seeing how you met hard situations
and dealt with the fear we all felt enabled us
to be able to do these and many other things.

We children have the knowledge that whatever we do you are supporting us. It has been
important to me to know that no matter what
kind of crazy flight I take off on, there is a solid
rock that supports me. I know that you would
do anything within your power to help me.

Looking back on the past twenty-five years,
especially the twenty-one I lived at home, I re-
alize that I have heard you preach hundreds of
sermons. Some were short, some long, but
most were in between, thank goodness! I do
not remember any particular one in great de-
tail, but I do remember something you often
said. And I want to relate this to you.

You have often said that when you die you
won't leave us a lot of money or material pos-
sessions, but you hoped you would be able to
leave us a good name. And you hoped that as
we viewed you for the last time we would be
able to say that there lies a holiness preacher
who lived what he preached and preached
what he lived.

I think that today as we honor you both for your forty years in the ministry, it is an appropriate time to tell you that I am proud to be a Harper. It is truly a good name, and I only hope I can pass it on to my family with the same luster that you gave it to us.

Also, since I was the last one of the kids at home, I can probably speak the best on your way of life. I can truthfully say that at home as well as in public you both live Christian lives and live what you preach and preach nothing that you do not live. You are truly a holiness preacher, and I am very proud of you.

Frank

You ask Rachel and me about our children and we will strut like a peacock and tell you we are proud and honored with the children. I'd fight a circle saw for any one of them.

When the invitations went out invit-*ing friends and family to attend the reception in 1978 honoring Tommie and Rachel on their fortieth year in the ministry, the children received notes from many church members and pastors with whom their parents had worked. These notes related events until then unknown by the children.*

Sister Jimmie White, a member of the first church Tommie and Rachel pastored, the Bridgeford Church of God, sent this account:

Two things Brother Harper did for us I shall never forget:

1. In the spring when Jessie would be plowing the corn with mule and plow, I would be dropping soda by hand. We did not have baby-sitters so Hubert and J. R. would stay at the end of the corn rows. Brother Harper would come by very often because it took several days and say, "Sister White, I will drop a few rows for you," and he would do several.

2. My grandparents lived about fifty or sixty miles away, and I had never attended Granddaddy's birthday celebration. I don't remember how they got to church for the parsonage was about a mile away from the church, but Brother and Sister Harper let us have their car to go to Granddaddy's birthday. It was the only one I ever attended.

Martha Hacker from the Rossville Church of God wrote:

There were six of us kids, including four boys who loved to play baseball. Daddy didn't make much money so we were not able to get special things. I remember the first spring after Brother and Sister Harper came to pastor. They had come to our house for fellowship. Brother Harper played a game of ball with the boys. And the only ball the boys had was one made by wrapping old socks together and then tying them with a string.

The next time Brother Harper came to visit, he brought the boys a brand new baseball.

Another member of the Rossville church, Catherine Bishop, sent the Harper children this account:

Carolotta tells about one particular Christmas. She wanted a certain doll—a bride doll—for Christmas. We had talked with her and told her she couldn't get it because it was too expensive. One day she was with the Harper family for Sunday dinner—she was about nine years old—and she was asked what she wanted for Christmas. She replied, "I want a bride doll, but Mother and Daddy told me to get it off my mind. And I do. But, Brother Harper, it keeps getting right back on there, and I can't help it."

When Christmas came the Harpers played Santa Claus and got Carolotta's bride doll for her. A happier little girl you had never seen.

Reverend Billy Olds, a pastor in Washington state while Tommie and Rachel were overseer there, wrote on the occasion of the 1978 reception:

Some years ago Reverend and Mrs. T. F. Harper came to the state of Washington as our State Overseer. . . . It seemed everywhere he went to preach he ignited fires in the churches. . . . Brother Harper stirred the heart of a young couple, Troy and Maye Johnson, at our church in Pasco. When Brother Harper told the congregation the need for workers in the city of Moses Lake, the Johnsons accepted the challenge. Incidentally, they are still there pastoring and have built a beautiful church there.

While preaching in Pasco one Sunday morning, unknown to Brother Harper, a young man was in the audience who was having serious marital problems and sin was wrecking his life. After hearing Brother Harper preach, the young man went to the hills across the river and bared his soul to God. This young man was my kid brother, O. V. Olds. Later on his wife was saved and their home brought back together again. Today they are pastoring in Amarillo, Texas, and God has greatly blessed their work!

One of his true "buddies in the Lord," Reverend Paul Stover, wrote to Tommie when he received his invitation to the reception in 1978:

Do you remember the time we became so burdened about a young man in the state of Nebraska, and we shared the expenses of the trip, drove all night and all day, or rather it was all day and all night, and got there around breakfast time the next morning? You talked with him while I took a nap in a chair, and I talked to him while you napped. We were in church services that night with him and left the next morning, not knowing if we had helped the young man or not.

We were back home about two or three weeks and got a letter from the young man. He had fixed everything up with the Church and General Headquarters, and we felt like shouting because we had helped save a young man for God and the Church.

You might say that 1979 was not a *very good year. In April Tommie became ill and was hospitalized, without much chance to live. He was sick for several months. In May Rachel's mother died unexpectedly on Mother's Day. And in July Elizabeth's young husband dropped dead on a six-mile jog near Tommie and Rachel's house on Possum Creek, two days before the Fourth of July. It was a time of heartbreak and pain.*

GOD IS ALWAYS THERE

We were in a dilemma. It was the spring of '79, and I was getting ready to plant the garden. Suddenly, I had a severe pain in my stomach. What followed was a long ordeal . . . two weeks in the hospital, some more weeks at home during which time I was supposed to get strong enough to go back to the hospital, weight loss from 223 to 150 pounds.

And now here were two doctors, talking across my hospital bed. Dr. Hoppe says, "If he's put on the operating table, he'll die." Dr. Dodds answers, "If he's not put on the operating table, he'll die in bed." So, with a stern warning to me and my family that they could promise nothing, the doctors agreed to operate.

When they left the room, I turned to the family and said, "Well, you heard them. We've got only a short little string. But we can all put our hands together and hold onto that string."

As I left for the operating room the next morning, one of the children said, "Daddy, don't forget. We're all holding onto that short little string. You'd better hold onto it too."

And hold on we did. God answered prayer and brought me through.

A strange thing happened during the first few hours that I was in intensive care after the operation. I had a vision. Mama, who had been dead since 1961, was coming up a path toward me. She had her little black pocketbook in her hand. When she was almost up to where I was, a man dressed in a long white robe stepped directly in front of her. She stopped, then made a step around him. He stepped back in front of her again. Then she looked around him as if to say something. He raised his hands over her. She turned and walked back down the path the way she had come, never looking back.

From that moment on there was an unbelievable change in my condition. The next day I was so improved that I was moved to a room where my family could be with me. It was a slow go, but the change was so profound that the doctors let me have my bed raised a little each day. After several weeks I came home, attesting to the great love of God. I was thankful to my friends for their prayers and untelling love. Someone told me later, "You couldn't have died. There were too many prayers for your healing."

THROUGH THE VALLEY OF
THE SHADOW OF DEATH

When Greg died that July, all I could think to say was, "God, why? Why?" I had always preached that we should never question God, but this was a blow that I could not understand. Greg was so young, only forty-three years old. He was so healthy. He had told me one day in May when he came to the hospital to see me that he and Elizabeth had just had their yearly physicals. He said, "Tommie, you know what the doctor said? He said, 'Greg, you have the best health of any man I've ever examined in Texas.'" Then Greg laughed and said, "The doctor asked me if my secret was that I did yoga. I told him, 'No, I just lead a good life.'"

And he did. He was one of the most loving people I had ever known. He and Elizabeth were so happy. I loved him like a son.

And now he was dead. The doctor said, "It was an imperceptible heart defect that he had had since birth—so small it would have never shown up in any test. He just had a heart that was going to last forty-three years, and that was that."

The afternoon he died he and Elizabeth had eaten supper with Rachel and me. They were at their cabin on the club grounds working on a book. Rachel and I were sitting outside on the porch about dusk talking with two men from the East Soddy church who had stopped by for a visit. A sheriff's patrol car pulled into the yard. The officer walked up to the porch.

"Do you have somebody visiting you from Texas?" he asked.

Rachel said, "Our daughter and son-in-law are here; they live in Texas."

"Can you come with me?" he asked and motioned to his car.

About that time a neighbor pulled into the yard; she had passed by the crowd down on the road. Rachel asked, "Is it Greg?" The neighbor nodded "yes."

We followed the officer's car. When we got to the curve right above the Possum Creek bridge there was a big crowd. An orange and white ambulance was parked in the gravel on the side of the road. Rachel and I got out. I pushed people away who were in front of me. "I've got to see," I said. "I don't believe it is him."

As I got close to the back of the ambulance, I could see inside. Elizabeth was sitting on a metal bench inside the ambulance door. She was staring straight ahead, holding somebody's feet in her hands. "Let me see," I said again. "I don't believe it is him."

The ambulance attendant pulled down the sheet. It was Greg.

*   *   *

Elizabeth and I went the next day to the lumberyard. We wanted to get some plywood to put down by the lake. That was where we were going to have Greg's memorial service. While we were standing in the lumberyard, Elizabeth said, "Daddy, we never thought we'd be buying plywood for this purpose, did we?" All I could do was shake my head.

*   *   *

The memorial service was beautiful. It was a bright, sunny day. The 4th of July. Everybody came to the grassy hillside down by the lake. We all sat in chairs and looked out over the water.

Frank conducted the service.

Several people spoke: David Stewart, Greg's department chairman whom he greatly loved; Skip Porter, one of Greg's best friends; Brother Hickman, our pastor. I never will forget what Frank said at the end:

> After hearing what Greg meant to all these people, if you can imagine that a hundredfold, you will begin to understand what he meant to his families.
>
> Greg-o enjoyed life to the fullest, and he did everything in his power to make sure that those around him enjoyed it also. One talent that Greg had that we should all try to emulate is his ability and willingness to express his feelings toward others.
>
> An example of this was just three weeks ago when everyone came to Atlanta for my graduation from law school. It was a joyous occasion, and everyone celebrated. And that night after Greg and Sister had gotten back to Texas, Greg called to let me know how much the day had meant to him and how much he enjoyed sharing it with me.
>
> Here today, before each of you, I pledge for myself that I will try to let each of you know what you mean to my life, and I

urge each of you to make the same commitment.

Then the congregation sang "I'll Fly Away" and "Amazing Grace." You could hear the sound echoing off the water and throughout the hills. I looked out at the lake at the end of the singing; a flock of ducks had swum up to the shoreline and were sitting there all in a row.

*   *   *

For weeks and weeks I could not get over Greg's death. I would pray and ask God to help me, but it seemed I could get no relief. One day after prayer, however, I felt led to look in the right-hand drawer of my desk. In there I found an article I had been saving since 1950 when I had first read it in *Reader's Digest*. It was a piece about the 23rd Psalm. An old Basque shepherd had interpreted the Psalm, and a reporter had written the interpretation down.

I took the article with me out on the porch, and I started reading it:

The Lord is my shepherd; I shall not want.

The shepherd said: "Sheep instinctively know that ere they have been folded for the night the shepherd has planned out their grazing for the morrow."

He maketh me to lie down in green pastures.

"Sheep graze from around 3:30 in the morning until about 10 o'clock," the shepherd said. "Then they lie down for three or four hours and rest."

He leadeth me beside the still waters.

"Every shepherd knows," said the Basque, "that sheep will not drink gurgling water. . . . Although the sheep need water, they will not drink from these fast-flowing streams. The shepherd must find a place where rocks or erosion have made a little pool, or else he fashions with his hands a pocket sufficient to hold at least a bucketful."

He restoreth my soul; He leadeth me in the paths of righteousness for His name's sake.

"Holy Land sheep exceed in herding instinct the Spanish Merino or the French Rambouillet," the shepherd said. "Each takes his place in the grazing line in the morning and keeps the same position throughout the day. Once during the day, however, each sheep leaves its place and goes to the shepherd. Whereupon the shepherd stretches out his hand, as the sheep approaches with expectant eyes and mild little baas. The shepherd rubs its nose and ears, scratches its chin, whispers affectionately into its ears. The sheep, meanwhile, rubs against his leg or, if the shepherd is sitting down, nibbles at his ear and rubs its cheek against his face. After a few minutes of this communion with the master, the sheep returns to its place in the feeding line."

Yea, though I walk through the Valley of the Shadow of Death, I will fear no evil. . . . Thy rod and Thy staff they comfort me.

"There is an actual Valley of the Shadow of Death in Palestine," the shepherd explained. "It is south of the Jericho Road leading from Jerusalem to the Dead Sea and is a narrow defile through a mountain range. . . . The valley is four and a half miles long. Its side walls are over 1500 feet high in places and it is only 10 or 12 feet wide at the bottom. Travel through the valley is dangerous because its floor, badly eroded by cloudbursts, has gullies seven or eight feet deep.

Actual footing on solid rock is so narrow in many places that a sheep cannot turn around. . . . About halfway through the valley the walk crosses from one side to the other at a place where the path is cut in two by an eight-foot gully. One section of the path is about 18 inches higher than the other; the sheep must jump across it.

The shepherd stands at this break and coaxes or forces the sheep to make the leap. If a sheep slips and lands in the gully, the shepherd's rod is brought into play. The old-style crook is encircled around a large sheep's neck or a small sheep's chest, and it is lifted to safety. . . .

Many wild dogs lurk in the shadows of the valley looking for prey. . . . The shepherd, skilled in throwing his staff, hurls it at the dog and knocks the animal into the washed-out gully where it is easily killed. Thus the sheep have learned to fear no evil even in the Valley of the Shadow of Death, for their master is there to aid them and protect them from harm."

Thou preparest a table before me in the presence of mine enemies.

"David's meaning is a simple one," the shepherd said. "Poisonous plants abound which are fatal to grazing animals. Each spring the shepherd must be constantly alert. When he finds the plants he takes his mattock and goes ahead of the flock, grubbing out every stock and root he can see. . . . in the presence of their deadly plant enemies, [the sheep] eat in peace."

Thou anointest my head with oil; my cup runneth over.

At every sheepfold there is a big earthen bowl of olive oil and a large stone jar of water. . . . As each sheep passes in single file [the shepherd] quickly examines it for briers in the ears, snags in the cheek, or weeping of the eyes from dust or scratches. . . . Each sheep's wounds are carefully cleaned. Then the shepherd dips his hand into the olive oil and anoints the injury. A large cup is dipped into the jar of water, kept cool by evaporation in the un-glazed pottery, and is brought out—never half full but always overflowing. The sheep will sink its nose into the water clear to the eyes, if fevered, and drink until fully re-freshed.

When all the sheep are at rest, the shepherd lays his staff on the ground within reach in case it is needed for protection of the flock during the night. . . . So, after all the care and protection the shepherd has given it, a sheep may well soliloquize in the twilight, as translated into words by David:"

Surely goodness and mercy shall follow me all the days of my life; and I will dwell in the house of the Lord forever.

The old Basque shepherd told the reporter:

"Our guild takes this poem as a lode-stone to guide us. It is our bulwark when the days are hot or stormy; when the nights are dark; when wild animals surround our bands."

When I finished reading, I felt a flood of peace. I had walked through the Valley of the Shadow of Death. Yes, and God's rod and staff were with me. And from that day on I was a different man. God helped me with my grief. I still miss Greg, but God has even helped me with that. Some days when I'm down on the lake fishing I almost feel Greg there beside me. I don't ever see him, of course, but it seems like his presence is there.

* * *

A year after Greg died, a very strange thing happened. Rachel and I were driving to church about 6:30 on Sunday afternoon. When we got to the exact spot where Greg had fallen, there came a young man jogging, just as Greg had been when he died. He was facing us on the exact same side of the road. As we passed him, we noticed he had a dark beard, close-cut, just like Greg's. It was such a feeling, seeing him right at the spot where Greg had died, resembling Greg so much—and on the day that was the first anniversary of his death. Neither of us said a word at the time. The moment seemed almost sacred like.

OUR GRANDCHILD IS BORN

Rachel and I had been married almost forty-five years when our grandchild was born. She was born on a Monday afternoon about 3:20 on June 30, 1980, in Decatur, Georgia. Frank called and told us. What a great thing to hear. Of course, we wanted to know all about her, and Frank gave us all the details of length and weight. We were so happy.

Rachel was down in the garden with me late that afternoon, and she said, "Frank said they were going to name the baby Sarah. But he didn't know what her middle name would be. What do you suppose they will choose?"

I said I didn't know. We worked on in the garden.

In a few minutes Rachel said, "You know what I think would be a pretty middle name for the baby?"

I said, "What?"

She answered, "I think a beautiful name would be Sarah Lynn."

Imagine our surprise the next day when Frank called to tell us the baby's full name: Sarah Lynn. I had an even deeper appreciation for Rachel after that!

*   *   *

We got to keep Sarah for a whole weekend when she was about eight months old. We enjoyed her so much. We put a quilt on the floor for her to play on, and at night Rachel fixed Sarah up in the big bed with pillows all around her so she wouldn't fall off. But even then Rachel would go in the baby's room and check on her all through the night.

When we took her to church on Sunday, we had to bring her home after Sunday School. She wasn't used to the singing, and we weren't used to tending to a little baby—so maybe the fault was ours more than hers!

Rachel also enjoyed putting Sarah in her stroller and walking around the club grounds and on down to the boat dock where I was fishing. We put the baby in the boat and took her picture. We had such a great time.

Rachel also likes to talk about Sarah.
Not long ago she wrote:

> I wonder what Sarah is doing today in California? She is probably waiting for her daddy to come home so she can go swimming in the great backyard swimming pool. She is energetic and full of life, and she talks so sweet and sensible. She loves to ride in an airplane and has been doing so since she was nine months old. She told us the other day when we were talking to her on the phone that on her last plane ride she listened to music and saw a movie and that she was fine and was five years old. She is real smart and writes us little notes of crosses and circles— her hugs and kisses, as she calls them. We have lots and lots of pictures of her around the house in all kinds of different poses. We know she is going to grow up to be a great person, as she is enveloped in love and care and concern in her everyday life.
>
> Sarah is looking forward to going to school this fall. She loves to read and has quite a collection of little books and picture books. She also loves to listen to tapes on her cassette player and just enjoys life all around. She is very intelligent.
>
> Just a word of warning: "Children, you better watch out! A champion is entering the school world this fall!"

HOW I COMMUNE WITH GOD

First of all, we were told when we got saved that if we would put God first in our lives that He would supply all our needs. This has always proven true.

I learned a great lesson in the first church we pastored. There was no money so a farmer that worked the big field in front of our house gave us corn to trade for groceries when the grocery bus came by on Friday. There was a fence between me and the cornfield. I had to cross the fence to get the corn. God had laid on the farmer's heart to give me the corn to buy groceries, but I had to climb the fence to get the corn. This is God working from both sides.

I personally believe that you do not have to tell anyone of your need, that God knows even before we have time to ask or think. Don't try to make it happen. Just let it happen.

I've never started a garden without first praying about it. I'll tell God, "This is your garden. I'm just working it. You must send the rain at the right time. Help me keep the bugs off the plants."

And all the while you are plowing, hoeing, poisoning the bugs on all the garden. And you always remember that there are two parts to the garden. The ten percent that belongs to God and the ninety percent that belongs to you and God.

In my fishing I first pray, "God, where is the best fishing in the lake today? Then while I'm out on the waves, I'm still remembering to put God first. Many times I have prayed until I felt as if I could get out of the boat and walk on the water! I did not do it; I only felt like it! And many times, after I've put my four rods out and am just sitting there talking to God, I'll have to say, "Lord, excuse me just a minute. I've got to land this fish. I'll be right back and pick up where we left off."

* * *

What I want most in life is always to have the work of the Lord and the Church of God come first and foremost. As far as I'm concerned, there is no place to quit. It's been the most satisfying thing in my life.

The thing I'm most looking forward to is the coming of the Lord. (I have a saying that I would like to be in a graveyard, crying, when Jesus comes. You ask me why? The answer is,

"God will wipe all the tears away." (Revelations 7 : 17) What could be greater than that!!)

As far as I'm concerned—even with the good family we have—my hope is strictly and forcibly in the thought of the rapture. As much as I love the family and see the goodness of the Lord on their part, my hope is still in the coming of the Lord and the rapture of the Church. That's when we'll have a chance to enjoy continually what we've enjoyed off and on all through life.

* * *

One of the saddest things for me in my late life is the change in the Church. Now it is quite common to find church members who are doing the same things they did, going to the same places they went to before they were saved. This just can't be. Our churches are flooded with those that believe that if you don't think it's wrong, it's not wrong.

God's plan is repentance, turning from your wicked ways. Then He said He would forgive your sins and heal our lands. Jesus came preaching, "Repent." John's message was, "Repent, for the kingdom is at hand." Sure, you can fill the church, but it will be of the world.

When I'm off by myself where I can really get in thought, I go back over my life. I go back to the early days and bring those memories up. I look at what the Church is today and what it was then and where the differences started and where they stopped—except they have never stopped yet. I meditate on these things. It makes me very sad. You can't give advice today as an old preacher because there isn't anybody to give advice to. They don't want to hear it. They won't take it.

Rachel talks about the relationship
she and Tommie have had with God over the years:

> I feel that living for the Lord day by day Tommie and I matured. As we encountered problems and worked them out through His word, we grew. The next time the trials came along, we could look back and see that the Lord had helped us through them and could know that He would do the same again. It was never in exactly the same way—sometimes we had to wait a long time to see our prayers answered. This was to teach us *patience* and *dependence* upon him. Sometimes our prayers were answered instantly. This increased our *faith* and *belief* in His word. Some of our prayers haven't been answered as yet, but we are *encouraged* and *ever expecting* them to be answered—thus still going through the maturing process.
>
> If things didn't go as we would like many

times in the work of the Lord, He would give us *grace* to stand still and wait on Him. He would always give us the *strength* to overcome obstacles if we fully depended upon Him.

As there can be no valleys without mountains, there can be no maturity without obstacles, but God is always there.

It is September of 1985. Tommie Harper is now 77 years old. Sitting with one of his children on the back porch, he says, "Let me show you the Scriptures I am using for my healing."

And he began to read aloud:

II Chronicles 20 : 15;17

Be not afraid nor dismayed by reason of this great multitude; for the battle is not yours, but God's.

Ye shall not need to fight in this battle:
Set yourselves, stand ye still, and see the salvation of the Lord."

Then he said, "Now, here's a verse for the individual:"

Ask, and it shall be given you; seek, and ye shall find; knock, and it shall be opened unto you: For

every one that asketh receiveth; and he that seek-
eth findeth; and to him that knocketh it shall be
opened. (Matthew 7:7−8)

*And, finally, Tommie turned in his Bible to He-
brews 4:14−16, and he read:*

Seeing then that we have a great high priest, that
is passed into the heavens, Jesus the Son of God,
let us hold fast our profession.

For we have not an high priest which cannot be
touched with the feeling of our infirmities; but
was in all points tempted like as we are, yet without sin.

Let us therefore come boldly unto the throne of
grace, that we may obtain mercy, and find grace
to help in time of need.

"Find grace to help in time of need . . ."

*That time was to come sooner than Tommie might
have thought. For just five weeks later, in mid-October,
without warning, Tommie Harper found himself in the
hospital emergency room. Diagnosis: cancer.*

THE LINE WAS ALREADY STRUNG

That night, the doctor did not want me to go to sleep. "I don't think, Reverend Harper," he said, "that you know how sick you are. If you go to sleep, you are likely not to wake up." He could not understand why I was not afraid. Plain in his talk, he asked, "Do you know how close to death you are?" I responded, "If this is death, I have nothing to fear."

When the specialist told me I had cancer, this did not scare me. The children called when they heard the news. "Daddy, are you worried?" they asked. I responded, "I'm not worried, and I'm not afraid." And that was the truth.

The doctor said, "We must operate right away." Rachel and I said okay. The next day I asked Rachel to bring me a book from home, *The Chemistry of the Blood and Other Stirring Messages*. A medical doctor, who was also a preacher in Grand Rapids, Michigan, wrote these sermons way back in 1943. His name was M. R. DeHaan. I have studied this book for years.

When Rachel brought the book, I turned to the chapter on "The Chemistry of Prayer." I read sections I had marked over the years:

> Prayer is everybody's gift and privilege. Whereas we often need preparation and training to become efficient preachers and personal workers, the gift of prayer is offered to all, and all may become the wielders of the very powers of Omnipotence.
>
> Not all men are called to be pastors or preachers or teachers or evangelists or exhorters. God gives to every man his gift and his task, according to his ability. But no such restrictions are placed upon the art of prayer. This gift is for all.
>
> Jesus says, "Men ought always to pray, and not to faint." Study the prayers of the Lord Jesus and you will discover . . . that He was a man of great prayer. He spent whole nights on the mountain without sleep, praying to God. . . .

I turned to the section of the sermon that talks about the three kinds of prayers:

> [The] three elements of complete prayer have been called—1. Communion 2. Petition 3. Intercession. . . .
>
> Communion does something *to* us, whereas in petition we have something done *for* us, and by intercession we have something done *through* us. . . .

> Communion strings the line. Petition throws
> the switch and Intercession connects others
> with your machinery of prayer and power. . . .

I had marked these lines in the section on
Communion:

> Communion is that part of prayer that re-
> moves every hindrance between God and our-
> selves. It is that act of worship and adoration
> which seeks only the glory of God. . . . It is the
> attitude of complete submission. . . . Commu-
> nion establishes the CONTACT so that our peti-
> tions can reach Him and our intercessions . . .
> can be heard and answered by God. Commu-
> nion is the line that connects our soul with
> the battery of God's power. A line must be
> strung from God's heart to ours before the
> power can flow into our lives.

Then there was a part that I have almost
memorized over the years:

> .   If we keep the lines clear and allow nothing
> to come between us and the Lord, then when
> a crisis comes and we need something quickly,
> we can just turn on the switch of Petition and
> get what we will. . . .
>   Keep the line open and then suddenly in
> sickness, temptation, trial, or even in the
> shadow of death, you can turn to Him and get
> what you need. . . .

I was glad my line was already strung.

I then turned to the section of Petition because today I needed something done *for* me:

"*. . . if there is unconfessed known sin in our lives the Lord will not hear us.*" I checked on that, and all was clear.

"*. . . an unforgiving spirit against a brother will hinder our prayers from being answered.*" I checked on that, and made sure that was clear.

"*. . . the Lord expects us to answer some of our own prayers.*" Well, I didn't think this time that applied to me because I wasn't a doctor so there wasn't much I could do.

"*. . . are you afraid that God will not answer your prayer?*" No, that certainly wasn't the case.

"*Friend, is the line up? Is the connection clear? Are you right with God and trusting Him? Then whatsoever ye shall ask of Him, it shall be done.*"

I finished reading. I handed the book to Rachel and said, "Put it back in the bureau drawer. God is going to take care of me."

The operation occurred on October *17, 1985. Eight days later Tommie was home. The doctor told the family, "It's his attitude and his trust in God that make the difference." At Thanksgiving Tommie and Rachel flew to California to celebrate their fiftieth wedding* *anniversary. On December 15, Tommie Harper was back in the pulpit, preaching the morning sermon at the Rossville, Georgia, Church of God.*

Tommie is an avid reader. The book *he reads the most is the Bible. Over his desk are three shelves on which he keeps the other books that are his favorites. These have been separated from the dozens of books he has in other parts of the house. An inventory of these shelves shows books like* With Signs Following; Touching Incidents and Remarkable Answers to Prayer; Hidden Manna; The Life of Charles G. Finney; A Pitcher of Cream: Sermons by Bud Robinson; Preacher and Prayer; Peter Cartwright: Backwoods Preacher; Sam Jones' Sermons: Lightening Flashes and Thunderbolts; Sermons by Reverend Sam Jones and His Life; The Chemistry of the Blood and Other Stirring Messages; *and* Outline Studies in Christian Doctrine. (Outline Studies *is one of Tommie's old textbooks from Bible School.)*

To the side of his chair Tommie keeps his favorite magazines: Field and Stream, Sports Afield, The Progressive Farmer, *and* The Farm Journal. *There is usually a western book that one of the children has sent him lying by the chair also.*

From his reading over the years Tommie has collected sayings he likes. Most of these he has written on small slips of paper and put in one or another of his Bibles. Here he pulls some of them together, adding a few of his own.

MOTTOES I HAVE LIVED BY

The following are some of the many sayings and quotes I have used in my ministry. Some are borrowed from great preachers of yesteryear. Some I have found in various places. Some are my own.

Today is the first day of the rest of your life.

I have already survived the most dangerous day of my life.

Instead of complaining because you don't get what you want, be thankful you don't get what you deserve.

Those who go against the grain of God's law shouldn't complain when they get splinters.

What is the one thing which causes you the greatest difficulty in your daily living? Insecurity, fear, guilt, worry, lack of direction.

JUST SUPPOSE

JUST SUPPOSE the Lord would begin tomorrow to make people as sick as they claim to be on Sunday.

JUST SUPPOSE the Lord should take away the child whom the parents use as an excuse for staying away from church.

JUST SUPPOSE the Lord should make people as poor as they claim to be when asked to help finance his program.

JUST SUPPOSE the Lord should have everyone stoned to death for covetousness as was Achan.

JUST SUPPOSE the Lord should let some parents look into the future and see what their example did for their children.

JUST SUPPOSE all Christians really loved the Lord!!

JUST SUPPOSE and then by the help of the Lord, go forth and live and serve as if eternity was soon coming!!

You cannot prove that this is not your last day on earth. If you believed that, you would get ready to meet your God!!

Whether you are a Christian or not, you must all be present on the judgment day.

If you want to find whether a man is crooked or straight, put a straight edge on him, The Bible.

I throw out a few bones for them to grow on and growl about.

Lord, give me faith.
Faith, like the old farmer with a hoe in his hand asking God for an ear of corn on every stalk.

Noise is not power. If it were, the devil is a mile ahead now. When you shout, be sure that it is real. A lie is a lie even if it is told or acted in the church. BE SURE.

If you can remember what you were and where you came from before God saved you, you would never have any trouble staying away from worldliness.

If we love, then let us show it.

There are rivers of difficulty between us and everything that is worthwhile.

God put the gold down in the heart of the earth, the pearls close to the bottom of the sea to make man search for them!!

If you repeat a story, ask yourself, "Is it true? Is it fair? Is it necessary?" If not, SHUT UP.

If there is no prayer in the pew, there will not be much power in the pulpit.

Remember the preacher is a physician without a pill, a surgeon without a scalpel, a lawyer without a license.

I get up in the morning and read the paper obituary and if I don't find my name then I wash my face in love and go to the table for breakfast. (George Burns)

The Vermont farmer was sitting with his wife one evening enjoying the sunset. It was a peaceful scene. After a long silence, the farmer spoke. "Sarah," he said, "we've had a lot of ups and downs together during these forty years, and when I've thought of all you have meant to me sometimes it has been almost more than I could do to keep from telling you!"

CELEBRATING OUR FIFTIETH WEDDING ANNIVERSARY

On October 13, 1985, Rachel and I celebrated our fiftieth wedding anniversary. The first celebration was in the hospital. Even there we had a festive occasion. The hospital staff gave us flowers and a cake, Barbara and Will drove down from Cleveland to be with us, and all the children sent gifts.

Then at Thanksgiving time the children pooled their resources and flew us to Frank and Sheri's in California. We spent a great week with them and Sarah. On the Saturday after Thanksgiving we had a celebration. Family, friends, and neighbors came.

One of the highlights of the afternoon was getting to visit with Bob and Donna Moore. It had been almost twenty-five years since we worked with them in Washington and Arkansas. We had many happy times together back then.

The entire day was good—the food, the weather, the company, the gifts and messages. We received remembrances from across the nation. We even received a card from the President of the United States!

Rachel said to me that night, "This has been a wonderful fifty years, and I wouldn't trade it for anything in the world."

"We've had a good life," I told her, "It has lasted through the ups and downs of fifty years."

* * *

I really appreciate Rachel's role in our ministry. She has been such a great help in my work. She always was a keeper at home. The children looked to her, as she was with them much of the time. She kept the home fires burning with a fine hand. When the time of discipline came, she would take care of it. She always took care of anything that needed to be done.

She was always helping people in the church. Sometimes she got so tired of the telephone ringing, but she was always there to talk. Every time we would sit down to eat supper—it almost never failed—old Sister Elmore would call to talk to Rachel. Many times she would also want Elizabeth to play her a piano solo over the telephone. So supper would wait while Mother held the phone and Elizabeth played Sister Elmore's request—the same one every night: "Precious Jesus, Hold My Hand."

Sometimes we'd be in a revival which would last for six, seven or eight weeks. The evangelist would always stay in our home. There was one revival which I remember especially. It had gone for five weeks, and Rachel was tired. She couldn't say anything, but I knew she was tired. She'd cook three meals a day and fix another one after church, keep up the house, keep the children ready for school and us all ready for church, and go to church each night. Of course, there was the washing and ironing, and answering the telephone and encouraging the believers, and many times going visiting with me.

We thought sure the five-week revival would close on Sunday night; but, alas, for Rachel, it went on. The Lord gave her strength and encouragement, however. The girls would take their schoolbooks to church and finish up their homework before church started.

When I served as state overseer, Rachel was a great help in the work. She took care of the office work while I was working with the churches. With untiring effort she worked through each prayer conference, camp meeting, and youth camp.

Since we retired in 1974 she has been an evangelist's wife. And she has nursed me back to health when I needed that.

I was kidding Rachel the other day. I said, "It sure is a good thing I married a younger woman. Now I'll have somebody to take care of me in my old age." (Rachel is ten years younger than me.) She told me to hush.

After fifty years with the same woman, you know you can count on her. I love and appreciate Rachel.

HOME FOR CHRISTMAS

We always look forward to the children coming home for Christmas. Our family is small, but they are scattered over the nation. They always "find their way home" for Christmas, though.

Weeks before, plans and preparations are made. The fruitcakes are baked and stand aging in the freezer. Pumpkin and sweet potato pies are baked and frozen for later use. Nearer Christmas, I buy bushel boxes of fruit—tangelos, honeybells, apples. Other cakes are made—sometimes Frank's favorite, German chocolate; other times, Barbara's and Elizabeth's favorite, a strawberry cake. The dried apples are already cooked and ready to make fried pies; Rachel will say, "I can almost see Jere's and Will's mouths watering now." And then Rachel will make spiced pecans from Sheri's recipe, and the "sweets department" will almost be complete. (There's always the Irish potato candy that Frances, Rachel's sister, makes that gets added to the collection when she arrives.)

We usually get our Christmas tree at the little fruit stand in Soddy. Rachel's job is to decorate the tree, and she loves it! Some of the decorations are handmade and many years old. Each one has its own story behind it, and Rachel tells the stories to me every year.

She travels a lot with the children, and she'll say, "Here's a little wooden auto from Detroit, a calico heart and ear of corn from New York City, a stuffed "human bean" from Seattle, a clay tree from Santa Fe, a boat from Texas, a gull from Newport, Oregon."

And then there are decorations made by Barbara's school children, and all the beautiful crocheted snowflakes made by my sister Blanche. No wonder it takes Rachel forever to trim the tree.

Finally, the tree is decorated, lights strung on it, and the switch is flipped. Whoops, a bulb is burned out! It is replaced and the tree is complete. (We have had the whole tree to fall after Rachel got it decorated. I get the credit when that happens. "You didn't anchor it well enough in the stand," Rachel will complain. And we can always count on the children saying, "Look at how that tree leans!")

My job every Christmas is to make a wreath out of fresh cedar branches to hang by the front door. We always hang lights and a Santa Claus face on the little tree in the front yard, too. I'm in charge of that. I enjoy doing both of these things.

We can hardly wait for the children and Frances to arrive, some by plane and some by automobile. Frances drives up from Brooks. Elizabeth and Jere come from Texas. They have their own business there. She is an author and has several best-selling books on writing. Jere is a businessman and publisher.

Barbara and Will drive in from Cleveland, Tennessee. They are teachers in the public schools. Barbara is a leader in education in the state of Tennessee. She recently completed her term as President of the Bradley County Education Association—the same year Will completed his term as President of the Cleveland Education Association.

Frank and Sheri fly in from California. Frank is a member of the American Bar Association. Since April 1985 he has worked as an executive, managing the Los Angeles branch of Zep Manufacturing Company. In early 1986 he was promoted to Regional Manager for Zep, covering Southern California and Arizona. Sheri is an architectural designer who works for IBM.

When everybody arrives, the gifts piled beneath the tree and all around it are a sight to behold. On Christmas Eve we always have our family program. Each member takes part—singing, acting out a skit, reciting a poem or a story, and reading the Christmas story. After our program we give out our stocking stuffers. We enjoy these about as much as our big presents. On Christmas morning the gifts are distributed. Of course, many, many pictures are taken. Each family will have its own camera. Then we have a Christmas breakfast of sweet potato biscuits and butter, a favorite of the family.

December 20th is Barbara's birthday and Christmas day is Elizabeth's, so at sometime during the holidays we have a "Happy Birthday" party for them.

One meal during the holidays is set aside for an old-fashioned country dinner—black-eyed peas, collard greens, corn bread, sausage pie, sweet potato pudding.

It's usually really cold at Possum Creek during Christmas time. The lake is frozen over, and the wind whipping off the lake sends cold chills. Sometimes there's snow which makes a beautiful picture of all the trees on the club grounds.

We take down the tree decorations and all the decorations around the house when everybody goes home. Rachel wraps each ornament in tissue paper and packs them in boxes. She then puts everything away till next Christmas. I tell her every year, "Now, Rachel, this year put those decorations somewhere where we can find them!" But we still have to hunt for them the next December!

Needless to say, Rachel and I are very lonesome after everyone has gone. But when the letters from the children start coming in the next week, we know we'll make it until next Christmas!

Tommie wrote this short story a day
*or two after Christmas 1985. He mailed it in one of
Rachel's letters to the children. The story illustrates that
Tommie is still Tommie . . . even after all these years.*

A TRUE SHORT STORY

They had enjoyed a great Christmas with lots of good things to eat. The day after Christmas, they had a fair breakfast—two pieces of toast, one piece of sausage, and coffee.

At noontime, while sitting in his chair enjoying reading and watching t.v., he was asked, "Do you want one or two cheese sandwiches for lunch?"

The answer was, "I don't want either one; but if I have to have a cheese sandwich, don't give me over one."

They eat the sandwich in peace, although this was not a very good follow-up after Christmas.

Later, the cook came through and said, "I will fix you some quail for supper. Does that sound good?"

So, they had their meal: liver for one and quail for the other.

Now they are living happily, waiting for breakfast. Just waiting.

Rachel, Tommie, and Sarah.

Rachel and Tommie's 50th wedding anniversary.

The house at Possum Creek.

THE PRESENT

Because he hath set his love upon me, therefore will I deliver him: . . . He shall call upon me, and I will answer him: I will be with him in trouble; I will deliver him, and honour him. With long life will I satisfy him, and shew him my salvation.

Psalms 91 : 14—16

At seventy-eight Tommie continues

to preach. *When you ask him how he feels, he reports: "The best I've felt since '79!" He often preaches for Reverend Lewis Hickman at the East Soddy Church of God or for Reverend Lewis Stover at Rossville or Reverend Burton Oliver at Chattanooga Valley. These men and Tommie remain close to each other in the Lord. When he visits Texas, Tommie preaches at the local Assembly of God church. When he and Rachel go visit her sister, Frances, he preaches at Frances' church. Other churches in the Chattanooga area continue to call on him. He is as busy as he wants to be.*

He also continues to grow his garden. Although the plot has decreased in size to what he can handle in his own yard, Tommie grows tomatoes, cucumbers, strawberries, and watermelons every spring. In the fall he plants turnip greens and sweet potatoes.

Hunting had to stop a few years ago when his bad knee began to keep him from the fields. But the fishing goes on.

AT HOME

Since we live on the lake, to go fishing all I have to do is just go down the hill to the boat dock, get the boat, and start. The lake is almost a mile wide at our landing. And we are only a mile or so from the Tennessee River, so we fish the river as well as the lake.

I have a fishing buddy, J. D. Mays. We are known as the two that can and do catch more fish than any of the others. Many times we come in with a five-gallon bucket full of fish in the fall and winter. We bring in eighty to a hundred yellow perch.

We live about a thirty to forty minute drive from a good place to eat and shop. During the winter, we are snowed in for days at a time here in the hills; but when you have plenty of good dry wood and two freezers full of food there is nothing to worry about. Our good neighbors Cleo and Lloyd Chambers make sure the wood always gets from the woodpile onto the porch.

I have some sweet potatoes in the ground now in our front yard. When the frost kills the flowers in the flower bed, I plant the sweet potatoes there. So all we have to do is go out our front door and start digging our sweet potatoes.

I also have a stalk or two of cotton growing in the yard. Rachel found a place in Waco, Texas, that sold a new kind of seed. I wrote them a letter asking if they would sell to an individual who only wanted a few seeds. They answered my letter—and enclosed the seeds! The cotton grows well here in the hills of East Tennessee.

We have dried apples on the front porch which Rachel and I fixed in the fall. And there's home-ground corn meal in the freezer. All is well.

We have faced some of the most try-ing times of our lives while living here at Possum Creek. But in all this we have found that God's promises are true: He has been with us through it all.

I know that I don't have the time in front of me that I have in the back. But God's promise that I hold on to is this: "I will never leave thee nor forsake thee." (Hebrews 13:5)

This I believe with all of my heart.

I don't know what tomorrow holds, but I know Who holds tomorrow.

To God Be The Glory

ACKNOWLEDGEMENTS

The following individuals are gratefully acknowledged for their financial contribution to publication of the Centennial Edition of **FROM THE PLOW TO THE PULPIT**:

David & Bobbie Alexander
Ken & Kathi Appelt
Imogene Bice
Joanne Black
J.R. & Ruby Butler
Reverend Cecil Campbell
Chattanooga Valley Church of God
Ray & Ann Cooper

Mrs. G.L. Curtis
Doraville Church of God
Gail Foote
Sharon & Dennis Hacker
Dr. Ernestine Hambrick
Frank & Sheri Harper
Reverend Robert Herrin
Rhonda Hobbs
Louise Holloway
Dick & Lil Jackson
Viola Jackson
Virgil & Nellie Kerley
Paul & Mildred Lambret
Frances Leach
Harry Mathews
Mike & Marion McMaster
Reverend & Mrs. Bertis Miles
Velma Mullens
Dr. William V. Muse
Elizabeth & Jerele Neeld
Reverend & Mrs. Burton Oliver
Earl & Jessie Pharr
Laura Reardon
James & Charlotte Robinson
Ruth Rominger
Bruce & Debbie Seay
Reba Smith
Bill & Sue Stewart
Reverend & Mrs. Lewis Stover
Reverend & Mrs. Paul Stover
Charles E. Thomas
Betty & Bob Unterberger
Tom Waldrep
Barbara & Will Walker
Carolyn Windsor
Reverend & Mrs. Parksie Wooten

The individuals below supported the picture research necessary to locate the photographs included in this book:

Frank & Sheri Harper
Tommie & Rachel Harper

Frances Leach
Blanche Harper Ninesling
Barbara Harper Walker

These people gave generously of their time to review the manuscript of **FROM THE PLOW TO THE PULPIT**:

Earl Babbie
Ralph Brewer
Charles Conn
Gerry Faulkner
Luis Gonzalez
Marcus Hand
Frances Leach
Mike McMaster
William Muse
Julia Poppy
David Stewart
Tom Waldrep

The following people are gratefully acknowledged for special support that made this Centennial Edition possible:

Mike Calloway
Charles Conn
Doraville Church of God
Gail Foote
Robert Herrin
Ray H. Hughes
Rossville Church of God
Reba Smith

These individuals and companies are acknowledged for the professional production of **FROM THE PLOW TO THE PULPIT**:

Jim Bendt, Back Cover Photograph
G&S Typesetters, Inc., Typesetting

Luis Gonzalez, Text & Cover Design
Rachel Harper, Manuscript Preparation
Rita King, Personal Services
Kinko's & On the Double, Photocopying
Eliot Lippman, Research
Parker Photo Processing, Text Photograph Preparation
Thornell Smith, Office Support
Pam Stoll, Front Cover Photograph
Walsworth Press Co., Inc., Printing

ORDER FORM

CENTERPOINT PRESS
Box 4771-B
Bryan, TX 77805
(409) 775-7887

Please send me _____ copies of FROM THE PLOW TO THE PULPIT.

NAME: _____

ADDRESS: _____

CITY: _____ STATE: _____

ZIP: _____

_____ books / $9.95: _____

Shipping: _____

(*Texas residents only*) Sales Tax: _____
(*Add $.51*)

TOTAL: _____

Shipping: Add $1 for the first book, and $.25 for each additional book

Enclosed is my check for: _____

Here is my VISA/Mastercard Number. Please charge my account.

VISA: _____

Mastercard: _____

Expiration Date: _____

Signature: _____

ORDER FORM

CENTERPOINT PRESS
Box 4771-B
Bryan, TX 77805
(409) 775-7887

Please send me _____ copies of **FROM THE PLOW TO THE PULPIT**.

NAME: _____

ADDRESS: _____

CITY: _____ STATE: _____

ZIP: _____

_____ books / $9.95: _____

Shipping: _____

(*Texas residents only*) Sales Tax: _____
(*Add $.51*)

TOTAL: _____

Shipping: Add $1 for the first book, and $.25 for each additional book

Enclosed is my check for: _____

Here is my VISA/Mastercard Number. Please charge my account.

VISA: _____

Mastercard: _____

Expiration Date: _____

Signature: _____